Man and Mason-
Rudyard Kipling

Richard Jaffa

authorHOUSE®

AuthorHouse™ UK Ltd.
500 Avebury Boulevard
Central Milton Keynes, MK9 2BE
www.authorhouse.co.uk
Phone: 08001974150

First published by AuthorHouse 05/31/2011

ISBN: 978-1-4567-8134-7 (sc)
ISBN: 978-1-4567-8152-1 (e)

Cover Design: Sue Mintz of Mintz Design

"The Craft's the trick, so help me!"
Rudyard Kipling
The Man Who Would be King

CONTENTS

Author's note: Although this book is primarily intended for Freemasons, there will be Kipling devotees who may wish to gain a better understanding of this aspect of his work. The author has therefore included in the Notes in the Appendix some explanation which will assist non-masons in understanding many of the Masonic references. Happily modern masonry does not suffer from the secretiveness that afflicted it in the last century and the author is always willing to explain (on email at rjaffa3266@aol.com), if he can, any references that remain obscure.

LIST OF ILLUSTRATIONS

Banner of Rudyard Kipling Lodge No. 8169, Battle, Sussex.

The Kipling Gavel from Grand River Lodge No. 151, Kitchener, Ontario, Canada.

Tyler's Book of Rosemary Lodge No. 2851, 17th November 1924.

Charity Accounts of Lodge Hope & Perseverance No. 782, Lahore.

Petition for Lodge, Builders of the Silent Cities No.4948.

Past Master Jewels of Lodge Hope and Perseverance No.782, and Lodge Independence with Philanthropy, No2, Allahabad.

Kipling Plaque from Sydney Harbour photographed by the author in November 2010.

I am grateful to the Grand Museum and Library of Freemasonry for permission to use the images of the Charity Accounts, the Petition and the Past Masters Jewels. Those images remain their Copyright. I must also thank the Worshipful Master and Brethren of Rudyard Kipling Lodge No.8169 for allowing me to reproduce their banner, to W. Bro.John Rogers of Rosemary Lodge for kindly finding the minutes of the one Lodge meeting that Kipling attended and to Grand River Lodge for the picture of the Kipling gavel.

PREFACE

This book owes much to the help and support I have had from many people. Firstly I would like to thank John Walker, the Honorary Librarian of the Kipling Society, for not only introducing me to the Society's Library at London University but also for devoting an immense amount of time reading my manuscript and making many helpful suggestions. Secondly I am hugely indebted to Richard Goddard, Rt. Wor. Provincial Grand Master of the Province of Worcestershire, who also read my raw manuscript and put me right on many issues. If any errors remain, they are entirely mine. Next I must thank Martin Cherry and his team at the Grand Museum and Library in Great Queen Street. Many of my most important discoveries were made there. I have written to many Lodges with Kipling links, and I am grateful for all the additional information and assistance they have given me, especially W. Bro. John Rogers of Rosemary Lodge No.2851. Finally my biggest helper, my wife Jane, whose tolerance and encouragement have always contributed to any project that I take on.

INTRODUCTION

This book grew out of a dissertation I wrote some years ago to get a master's degree. I had read *Kim* and a number of other novels about India as part of my degree course at the Open University, but until that point I had not realized that Kim's link to Freemasonry in the novel was the key to his identity, and how frequently references to Freemasonry appeared in Kipling's work. I therefore decided to research the influence that Masonry had on him and his writings. I found that I had embarked on a larger subject than I had expected. Although some of the ground had been trodden before, no-one had brought all the different elements together. Masonic writers were only interested in his limited career in the Craft and I felt they failed to analyse the impact of it on his writings, being purely content to identify the Masonic references. Literary critics and biographers, with no knowledge of Freemasonry, frequently made unwarranted or unsubstantiated arguments as to the reason for his interest, and usually tried to twist what little information they had, to fit their own particular interpretation of Kipling's work.

I hope that this book will be the first serious attempt to address both the Masonic and literary implications of Kipling's abiding interest in Freemasonry.

I admit that I had a head-start in tackling this subject. I became a Freemason in 1970 for no other reason than that my late father had obviously enjoyed his involvement in the Craft and my father-in-law was a Past Master of St. Paul's Lodge No. 43, one of the oldest Lodges in the country. I joined No. 43 and have now completed 40 years in the Craft. I have made many friends, not just in England but also in France and Germany where Freemasonry operates on a smaller scale, but often with more intellectual intensity. On the continent Freemasonry has links going back to the Enlightenment movement of the eighteenth and nineteenth centuries and European Freemasonry has been one of the beneficiaries of the collapse of communism.

Kipling remains an enigmatic and elusive figure. While he is generally judged a clear-thinking and straightforward writer, he was also a highly complex individual. He made it clear in his autobiography that he wanted to be judged on his work alone and that, both metaphorically and literally, is the essence of good Mason. In this work, Kipling's life and his interest in Freemasonry are inextricably connected

The deeper I delved into Kipling's life and his interest in Freemasonry and his output over more than half a century, the more the contradictions about him become apparent. Here was a man who suffered terribly in childhood and later lost two out of his three children in tragic circumstances, yet wrote enduring classic works for young readers. This same man, who was medically unfit for military service, was so devoted to British servicemen and their struggles that he became their greatest advocate and single-handedly raised their image for early twentieth century Britain. For many people in the last decade of the nineteenth century and the first of the twentieth, Kipling represented the spirit of the age. No author has generated so much affection among the ordinary working man and especially the country's soldiers and sailors. For more than two decades, he was the people's poet. Yet, in the last twenty five years of his life, he was almost rejected by the critics and British public, so that he became almost the forgotten man of British literature and his death produced only muted response and nominal tributes.

Why did the Nobel Laureate become almost irrelevant to the British public? Why did the critics largely ignore his later work, only for its significance to be recognized after his death? Why did his popularity decline to such a level? These are some of the questions that have only been partially answered. I hope to explain why his attachment to Freemasonry, which began as a twenty year old, permeates all his work and that, even with the minimal contact he had with the craft for half a century, it forms the bedrock of his thinking. One can see why the use of Freemasonry in his early work is largely a dramatic device but when he returns to it after the First World War he engages with it in a far more profound way, especially its key message of universal brotherhood.

Kipling's range, his style and his views on politics, women, the forces and life are quite unique. He could be conservative and reactionary in political terms but also modern and progressive in the immense interest and knowledge he displayed in the new technology and science in the first quarter of the new century. He was largely self-educated and he had no desire to be an intellectual. His preferred heroes were the men of action of his age. He believed that a man's legacy was his work and he should be judged by that.

My view is that much of Kipling's creed and his approach to man and God were derived from his early Masonic experiences. More than any major writer before or after him Kipling's life and work were governed by a moral code. He had studied and observed all the major religions and he appeared to reject the corset of formal religion but never ceased to seek a structure that would bring some order to the chaotic and often cruel world he saw around him. It was all encapsulated in what became Kipling's "Law".

His views on British Imperial power have been frequently used against him, but a closer examination of his work shows he was not a doctrinaire imperialist. He approved of the concept of the British Empire but not for any jingoist motive but for the force for good it seemed to be in the developing world. Imperialism may have become a discredited philosophy since the First World War, but 125 years ago it was a very different beast. Kipling should be judged by the standards of his time, not those of the twenty-first century.

I also think that under the vast weight of biography and literary criticism written about him since his death, his achievements and literary standing have been under-valued and that he merits a higher plinth in the pantheon of literary immortals. His work was shaped by his upbringing and early years in India and the perspective he acquired working as a journalist there. Critics have often forgotten the range of his work. Apart from the journalism and short stories of his youth, he wrote poetry, novels, political speeches, military history and children's books. He managed to combine the lightness and imagination required for children's stories with the darker work that marked his later years. He mixed his own experiences with his vivid imagination. He continues to intrigue us more than seventy years after his death. Perhaps he has frustrated all the critics and biographers, because ultimately they cannot fit him in one tidy pigeon-hole or theory. Like many other great authors his output was inconsistent and he had his bad patches. Bad Kipling could be awful but equally in many areas he was utterly original and without equal.

Kipling died on 18th January 1936, just two days before his friend King George V. The King's death overshadowed Kipling's cremation on the same day. On the day that the King's body was brought to London to lie in state, Kipling's ashes were interred at Poet's Corner in Westminster Abbey, next to Charles Dickens and Thomas Hardy. It was the end of a remarkable life which saw him rise from a junior reporter on a small Indian newspaper to become the first English Nobel laureate and the confidante of politicians, writers and monarchs.

Many of Kipling's contemporaries and several serious writers who sold widely in the 1920s and 1930s, have been largely forgotten, even by academics and students, but rarely a year goes by without a reappraisal of Kipling's life and work. His literary reputation has often appeared more like a battlefield.

During the last part of his life his political views often alienated all but his closest admirers so that, even when he was right, his opinions were ignored. Ironically, subsequent history has proved that many of his predictions were correct. His attitude to Germany before both World Wars now seems prophetic. Despite the relative decline in his public standing in the last fifty years, there is hardly a corner of the English speaking world where you will not find his influence today. In his lifetime his views impacted on politicians on both sides of the Atlantic and in Africa.

He started by chronicling colonial life in India at the apogee of the Raj. His writing about India in the 1880s is quite unique and unequalled. No-one captured life in nineteenth century India in manner of Kipling. Fame for him arrived early, and by his twenties he had already become a major literary figure. While working as a young newspaper reporter in India he became a Freemason. His active involvement in Freemasonry was brief but his writings reveal that the Craft influenced him for the rest of his life and his work contains many Masonic elements. In his more youthful writings Freemasonry adds mystery, intrigue and adventure to his stories, but in the darker short stories of the post First World War period it became an important tool to examine the effects of war on men, and the benefits of Masonry on these battle scarred soldiers as they came to terms with the horrors of the war.

Another result of his involvement in Freemasonry is the extent it helped develop the moral code - "Kipling's Law"- that permeates all his work. When you examine Kipling's work against the narrative of his life, it is abundantly clear that his early experiences affected him deeply and that there was very little of his life that was not reprocessed and translated in some form in his writings. Freemasonry supplied some of the building blocks that went into creating the distinctive Kipling mindset. Despite the many volumes written about him, much of his Masonic content has been ignored or missed. The number of prominent Freemasons among his close friends is another indicator that he remained close to the craft even when he was a non-participant.

Most Freemasons know that Rudyard Kipling was one of them, but few realise the extent to which it features in his work. I hope this will give them an opportunity to learn more about the man and how the principles of the Craft are woven into his thinking and narratives. I have assumed that Masons will not need Masonic terminology or ceremonies explained but, as I hope there will also be non-Masons who will read this, I have incorporated some explanation in the text as well as providing some notes at the end. Much of the information I have included here is available but it is very fragmented and dispersed over many different sources and I hope that I have brought it together in a manner that will help those interested in his Masonic connection to understand how it features in his life, affects his work, and the response it produced in the wider world.

I have read all the biographies of Kipling quoted in the bibliography at the end of this book but most of the chronology of his life is derived from Charles Carrington's authorized biography. Both in the Kipling Journal and the Masonic publication Quatuor Coronati there are many articles about Kipling's interest in the Craft and I have used these resources for which I am extremely grateful and hopefully have acknowledged the authors.

The values that Kipling espoused have not changed and I hope this volume will persuade some of my readers to visit or revisit some of his masterpieces.

Richard Jaffa LL.B., M.A.
Birmingham April 2011

Past Junior Grand Deacon of the United Grand Lodge of England, Past Assistant Provincial Grand Master, Province of Warwickshire.

CHAPTER ONE
KIPLING'S OWN STORY

Rudyard Kipling was born in Bombay on 30 December 1865. His parents, both children of active Methodist families, had met at a picnic at Rudyard Lake in Staffordshire. His father, John Lockwood Kipling, had trained as an artist and sculptor and was working for a pottery firm in Burslem in the Potteries when he met his future wife, Alice Macdonald. With no other inviting jobs on offer, he accepted an appointment at a new school of art in Bombay. They married and immediately set sail for India. Rudyard was born shortly after his parents arrived.

He was baptized into the Church of England, in Bombay Cathedral, as Joseph Rudyard. His mother was one of four sisters [1] all of whom made notable marriages. The MacDonald family had fled Scotland after Culloden and settled in Northern Ireland. Rudyard's maternal grandfather, George, became a Methodist minister.

Alice's sister Georgina married a man called Ned Jones – later to become Sir Edward Burne-Jones the leading pre-Raphaelite painter. "Aunt Georgy" was to provide an occasional home for the Kipling children during their parents' absence in India. Their bustling house in Fulham was a meeting place for leading artists and writers of that generation and from an early age Kipling mixed with some of the greatest contemporary figures in the arts, including William Morris and Robert Browning.

Another of Alice's sisters, Louisa, married Alfred Baldwin, a steel merchant from Worcestershire. Their son – Rudyard's cousin and childhood playmate, Stanley, later became Prime Minister. As adults, the cousins were to find themselves on different sides in political debate but Kipling retained his friendship. The fourth of the sisters, Agnes, also married an artist, Edward Poynter, who, as Sir Edward, became the President of the Royal Academy in 1896. These family connections played a major role in Kipling's life. During his childhood and schooldays the homes of his aunts were not only a refuge but also the point at which he first connected with the literary and artistic world.

Rudyard spent his first six years in India, apart from a trip to England at the age of three. This was to accompany his mother, who was sent home to give birth to her second child, Rudyard's sister Alice (known to everyone in the family as Trix). Rudyard's birth had been difficult and after that his mother returned to England each time she was close to her confinement. A third child died shortly after birth. A number of biographers have recorded that on one or other of these trips to England the young Rudyard upset his relatives with his unruly behaviour.

From his own description of his early childhood, it sounds idyllic. He was treated as a little sahib by the Indian servants and barely spoke English, becoming fluent in Hindustani. The warmth that Kipling enjoyed with the Indian servants as a child remained with him. He also seems to have started to grasp the complexity of India from his earliest days. His father was teaching at the School of Arts in Bombay and the whole family led a fairly comfortable existence, mixing increasingly with the higher echelons of the British Raj. For Rudyard this idyll came to an abrupt end. Like many parents, the Kiplings did not want to risk their children's education or their health to the climate and disease of India. The death rate among children (and adults for that matter) was appallingly high.

Cholera and typhoid extracted a very high toll on all age groups. Almost one third of British ex-patriots in India died from disease. Colonial parents wanted their children educated in England, not only for health reasons but also because many parents did not want their children to pick up the distinctive accents that could mark them in later life as Anglo-Indians.

Tough Times in Southsea

So, in 1871, when Rudyard was six and Trix was barely three, they were taken back to England. Their father had a six month vacation and at the end of that break, when the parents were due to return to India, Rudyard and Trix were placed in the care of a Captain and Mrs. Holloway at Lorne Lodge, Campbell Road, Southsea. They were given no warning of this impending move and separation from their parents. Why the Kiplings chose this establishment, instead of placing them with family members, has never been clear. It was traumatic- more so to Rudyard. Trix, much younger and a girl, was not treated as harshly as Rudyard and was probably too young to appreciate their initial situation. Trix later wrote that it was the lack of explanation that made it so hard to bear. Kipling called it "The House of Desolation."

It has been suggested that Rudyard had upset some of his elder relatives by being noisy and boisterous on an earlier visit to England, which had meant their help was not available. Perhaps Lockwood and Alice did not want to be dependent on the more successful members of their family. Rudyard spent almost six miserable years in Southsea, which he recreates in his story *Baa Baa Black Sheep.* [2] The events in the story closely parallel the sentiments he expressed in his autobiography. Some of his biographers consider that the treatment he received at Southsea affected his outlook for the rest of his life. "An immense and agonizing dislocation". [3] The critic Edmund Wilson had an even more radical view. He felt that this period of his life affected Kipling so much that his whole life "was shot through with hatred." [4] Kipling himself, however, asserts that the ordeal at Southsea had "drained me of any capacity for real, personal hate for the rest of my days", a view supported by his sister. [5]

There seems little doubt that Kipling appears to have suffered quite badly in the Holloway household. Having been treated like a little prince in India, this was quite a brutal contrast and he must have reacted badly to it. The Holloway's twelve year old son bullied him relentlessly and Mrs. Holloway was very free with the cane and other punishments. "An establishment run with the full vigour of the Evangelical as revealed to the Woman". [6] His eyesight, which was already poor, continued to deteriorate-something which went unrecognized for a lengthy period. Kipling himself, in his autobiography, leaves no doubt as to how awful it was. Captain Holloway tried to temper the misery endured by the youngster but Kipling wrote "I had never heard of Hell, so I was introduced to it in all its terrors - I and whatever luckless little slavey might be in the house, whom severe rationing had led to steal food."

He continues: "I have known a certain amount of bullying, but this was calculated torture - religious as well as scientific."[7] With the lack of spectacles and delayed diagnosis of his eyesight problem, it was not until 1874 that Kipling learnt to read. Once mastered, this then became his great consolation and to escape the misery he read everything he could get his hands on. As a relatively young child he was absorbing an eclectic range of books and magazines. He relates "And somehow or other I came across a tale about a lion-hunter in South Africa who fell among lions who were all Freemasons, and with them entered into a confederacy against some wicked baboons."[8] He later suggests that this distant memory was part of the inspiration for Mowgli and the Jungle books, which he started in 1892. In fact in 1897 he wrote to the publisher Edward Routledge, trying to trace the boy's annual which he had read as a child in about 1875.[9]

Kipling wrote about the story in his letter: "It concerned a man who wandered into the interior of Africa and there met a lion who (to the man's no small amazement) gave him a Masonic sign. On the strength of this little variation from the normal he struck up a friendship with the lion, his family and the rest of the lion-people and discovered that their deadly enemies were some dog-headed (and entirely unmasonic) baboons with whom he and the lions fought a furious fight." Professor Pinney was able to identify the story as *King Lion* written by James Greenwood. This had appeared in the *Boy's*

Own Magazine of 1864. It demonstrates his remarkable memory for detail.

It may be amazing that a child of no more than seven or eight should have that recollection, but Kipling himself said that what he read during his desolation in Southsea later formed the basis of the Jungle Books. He soaked up everything he could get his hands on, including the Bible. His facility for biblical quotations, and his capacity to remember what he had read and experienced, was acquired from that period. He kept his misery to himself (something that became a lifetime habit) and did not communicate it to his parents or the other relatives whom he visited during the holidays. He was sent to Hope House School, an inadequate school in Southsea, and that and the problems with his eyesight, held back his education. Trix suggests that their tragedy at Southsea "....sprang from our inability to understand why our parents had deserted us." [10]

While at the Holloway home, Kipling admits in his autobiography that he had some form of nervous breakdown, a problem which would periodically afflict him as an adult. However, for one month each year he and Trix had an escape from this misery when they went up to London to stay with their adored Aunt Georgy Burne-Jones at her home at The Grange, North End Road, Fulham. Away from the desolate suburban villa in Southsea they were enveloped in fashionable London artistic society. Their uncle was already becoming an important figure in the world of art and the Burne-Jones' house was filled with leading artistic lights. Among the acquaintances the Kipling children acquired was Uncle Topsy, (better known as William Morris) the leading figure in the Arts and Crafts movement. The children also met an aging Robert Browning who was a visitor to the house. It was his Aunt Georgy who realized that young Ruddy needed spectacles; once he had those his progress at school improved rapidly. Famously before he could read properly he had hidden one of his school reports, and when an outraged Mrs. Holloway discovered this she made him walk to school with a sign saying "Liar" on his back.

Eventually his mother returned from India and took her children away from Mrs. Holloway for a holiday in Epping Forest. That was the end of Rudyard's sojourn at Southsea although Trix returned there for several years more.

At School in Devon

So, finally, this unhappy period came to an end and Kipling was sent to the United Services College at Westward Ho!, Bideford Bay in Devon. Like many schools of that period it existed to provide a home and education for the children of colonial servants. Founded only in 1874, its main task was to prepare these boys for the services entrance examinations. It never ranked among the better schools, and it is unlikely that Kipling's parents could have afforded to send him to one of the top public schools. It provided a cheap education for the children of poorer colonial servants. Seventy five per cent of the pupils had been born outside England. "... it was primitive in its appointments, and our food would now raise a mutiny in Dartmoor." [11] Most boys were prepared for the services' examinations, but Kipling, with his poor eyesight, was never a candidate. Cormell Price (known as Crom), the headmaster, was an expert at preparing the boys for the competitive examinations for the services. The school, compared to other late Victorian public schools, bordered on the secular, as it required no uniform and religion was low on its priorities. Price had been at school in King Edward's in Birmingham with Edward Burne-Jones and was a family friend.

Kipling's schooldays are reflected in the stories of *Stalky & Co.*[12] These are a fictionalized version of this time, and this is corroborated to some extent by his two closest school friends Dunsterville and Beresford, who both later wrote widely differing versions of life at the school and of Kipling as a schoolboy. In the *Stalky* stories, the three leading characters are Stalky himself (later Major-General L.C. Dunsterville), who is clearly the leader of the pack, M'Turk (G.C.Beresford, who was an Irish nationalist and an engineer), and finally Beetle (the bespectacled Kipling-who was also called "Gigger"or " Giglamps"). Kipling and Dunsterville remained friends for the rest of their lives. At school and in the stories, just as Stalky was the leader, Kipling was the observer or spectator. The stories of schoolboy pranksters surprised English readers who had been brought up on the slightly higher moral tone of *Tom Brown's Schooldays*, *Tom Sawyer* and *Huckleberrry Finn*. To most literary critics the *Stalky* stories are considered fairly crude and not amongst Kipling's finer works.

Just as he had drawn on his childhood experience for *Baa Baa Blacksheep,* he again used his experience for the schoolboy tales. The school was a typical lower range English public school. That meant fagging, beatings, and plenty of cold baths. The boys were kept busy, as Crom Price believed in wearing out his pupils so that they would not be tempted to indulge in beastly practices!

Kipling's use of his personal experiences was something that was central to his writing, especially during his days in India. He developed the ability to take his personal experiences and use them for ideas, narratives or characters, adding the dramatic and imaginative dimension that made him such a successful story teller. No material was wasted; just as later he would utilize his Masonic experiences in many of his stories.

One of his breaks from school, apart from regular trips to London, was a trip to the Paris Exhibition in 1878. Kipling accompanied his father, who was in charge of the Indian exhibits there. Kipling developed a life-long love of France, which probably originated from this trip as a twelve-year-old. His father encouraged him to learn French - by no means a popular step at that time. From this point Kipling developed a great admiration for all things French, just as he later developed an equally great loathing for all things German.

After the bullying at Southsea, Kipling was partially protected at school by the fact that Cormell Price, the headmaster, was a close family friend. Accepting the fact that the short-sighted Kipling was hopeless at sports, Price encouraged the young Kipling to read, and gave him the run of the school library. He also gave him the editorship of the school magazine, and must take a great deal of credit for spotting the early literary potential of his pupil. Kipling began writing poetry while still at school and even had his first short story published under a pseudonym. In his brusque manner, he acknowledges in his autobiography the encouragement he was given by Price and other masters at school.[13] He edited seven issues of the school's magazine as well as contributing to other issues.

John Lockwood Kipling and Crom Price appear to have come up with the idea that Kipling should train as a journalist in India, and arranging for him to meet his prospective employer. It seems that the young Rudyard had very little say in the matter. The career choice was made chiefly by his father. Apart from the strong connection between Price and the Kipling family, it seems that during his remaining time at school, Price increasingly encouraged Kipling in preparation for his possible career.

It was during his time at school that, on a trip to visit Trix at Southsea (she remained there for a total of nine years), he met her friend Florence Garrard for whom he developed a great and enduring passion. It is possible that Florence was the model for many of the strong and independent women who later appeared in Kipling stories, of which the most obvious candidate is the character of Maisie in *The Light That Failed*.[14] His infatuation with Florence began while he was still only 14 and was to last nearly eleven years. Maisie, in the novel, bears many similarities to Florence. She was determined to become an artist, and achieved that without ever finding much success. She lived in Paris with another woman as a forerunner of the modern feminist. She never married and many biographers assume that she may have been a lesbian. Kipling's biographers have speculated on this relationship, which was carried on at long distance after he returned to India. Perhaps they make too much of it; he was a seventeen year old boy who had been away at boarding school and was possibly just a teenager with a crush on the first girl he had taken seriously. A more difficult question is why the relationship lasted as long as it did. There is no evidence of any reciprocation from Florence, and when eventually she brought it to an abrupt end, Kipling was clearly distressed.

As Kipling and his wife Caroline later destroyed much of his correspondence, records about the relationship are sadly lacking, but it is likely that Kipling had at least two other "engagements" including the sister of the woman who was later to become his wife. He also enjoyed attachments, almost certainly platonic, with a number of older women chief of these was Mrs. Edmonia Hill, who befriended him during his later period in India and with whom his correspondence was extensive and especially warm. His letters to her as a young man, burst with vitality, news and gossip, and he spent much time as a lodger in her house while in India. However, after the early death of her husband and while he was still single, he showed no interest in pursuing the relationship.[15]

India

The possibility of Rudyard going to Oxford or Cambridge does not appear to have been considered, though whether the family could have afforded that may have been a factor. Carrington, authorized as a biographer by Kipling's daughter Elsie, quotes a letter from John Lockwood Kipling which suggests that his father thought he would be better back in India as otherwise he might be tempted by the fleshpots and vices of London.[16] So, not yet seventeen, Kipling went back to India. He looked at least four or five years older than his years. He had always had a very swarthy complexion and even at that age could sport a healthy moustache, as contemporary photographs demonstrate.

At the time of Kipling's return to India, the horrors of the Mutiny of 1857 were still a vivid and recent memory for older British residents, but generally the administration controlled from London had reached its apogee. Kipling's next five years in the sub-continent were during its most halcyon days, before the rise of Indian nationalism began to assert itself more vigorously. At the time of his return the Governor General was George Robinson, first Marquis of Ripon (1827-1909) who, until he converted to Catholicism, had been the Grand Master of the United Grand Lodge of England from 1870 to 1874. Biographers have commented that Ripon had not appreciated the ideological differences between Freemasonry and his new church.[17] He was succeeded as Grand Master by the Prince of Wales, who later became King Edward Vll. Such was the public outcry when news of his conversion was announced, despite his success as Grand Master, that he had to resign hurriedly from his elevated position in Grand Lodge. In 1874 the Roman Catholic Church was still publicly hostile to Freemasonry, and being a Roman Catholic was still unpopular with the English establishment. In a biography of Ripon one of the chapters is headed *From King Solomon's Throne to the Pope's Footstool*.

The Mutiny had, of course, led to major changes in the relationship between Britain and India. The causes of the Mutiny were complex, but the overall result was that the East India Company's two centuries of rule was replaced by direct government from Westminster, and some twenty years later Victoria became Empress of India. There had been extreme violence on both sides, and it was the first time that both Hindus and Moslems had found common cause against the British. It would be another ninety years before India shook off control from London but the process towards independence had begun.

John Lockwood Kipling and Cormell Price, having decided that young Rudyard was ideally fitted to be a journalist , arranged an interview in London with his editor-to-be, Stephen Wheeler. He was found a job in Lahore on the *Civil and Military Gazette*. It was the Punjab's only daily newspaper, which put constant pressure on all its employees. Kipling, still only sixteen, became one half of its editorial staff and assistant editor. If the best training is to be thrown in at the deep end, he certainly had that.

He was happy to be back with his parents, with whom he still enjoyed a warm relationship, although he had hardly seen them for ten years. There is no suggestion that he bore any resentment for the miserable time at Southsea. This warm and enduring regard for his parents was a major contributor to his success and his father especially was a continuing influence on his work. By this time his father had become Principal of the School of Architecture and Art, and Curator of the Museum in Lahore. Kipling, at home with the family, enjoyed the comforts available to most ex-patriots in India. He had his own servants. He was paid the princely sum of 100 rupees - about £6 - a month. Throughout this first period back in India he seems to have continued his understanding with Florence Garrard, which lasted until she formally terminated the relationship in 1884.

Stephen Wheeler, his Editor, worked him hard, but Kipling later admitted his debt to him. As the teenage assistant editor of a provincial daily newspaper he had to read all the daily telegrams from the news agencies and sub-edit readers' contributions, as well as writing copy and proof reading. Before he became seventeen, he even took temporary charge when his editor was sick. He learnt shorthand and gradually reported more significant events. Later he spent six months in Simla (where the

Viceroy's Government spent the summer) acting as the newspaper's special correspondent. This period provided the material for what became his first set of short stories. The arrival later of a new editor, Kay Robinson, gave the fast maturing Kipling the chance to display his talents. He joined the local "club", the Punjab Club, which was the centre of existence of the unmarried English ex-pats.

He dined regularly at the Club and here he met the colonial administrators, running the railways and the schools, together with military men, engineers and other professionals. He rapidly absorbed and understood the hierarchy of the Raj. He was sent to cover all the newsworthy events in the area. Wheeler not only worked his apprentice hard but sent him to cover a wide range of stories and closely monitored his output. After work in the hot and humid nights in Lahore, Kipling rambled around many parts of the city and learnt more about Indian society at first hand than most Anglo- Indians. Lahore was a predominantly Moslem city and key to the prosperous Punjab.

Just as his childhood in Southsea affected his outlook, his wide experience in India as a young man, as an observer of both European and Indian culture, impacted on him even more. He entitled this chapter in his autobiography "Seven Years Hard". Life certainly was hard and death more commonplace than at home in England. The sources of cholera and malaria were still unknown in 1883. Kipling describes how during the heat of the summer "sudden causeless hates flared up between friends..."[18] The Anglo-Indians became inured to the frequent demise of young people and this is reflected in Kipling's Indian stories. Death is sometimes poignant but it is nevertheless an every-day event in India to be accepted philosophically.

When he returned to Europe he found the distress caused by death hard to accept after the relative indifference with which it was often greeted in India. His own losses and the First World War would radically change his perspective on death and bereavement.

The major benefit of being back in India was the unity of the family group. After Trix returned from England, the Kiplings enjoyed a congenial period of four years as a family and the strength of the family quartet was a crucial key to Kipling's character. Father, mother, son and daughter all had exceptional and complementary talents and supported each other in their respective interests - both in India and later in England. His parents were both popular and in demand socially and moved at a higher level within the Raj than their respective stations would normally permit.

One of the delights of his work in India was the connections that he struck up with the soldiers at every level. He met many officers, right up to the level of the Governor General, but he also met the men of the lower ranks who would become the raw material for some of his best Indian stories. "I came to realize the bare horrors of the private's life....". [19] Among the characters he created in this period were the Soldiers Three – Mulvaney, Learoyd and Ortheris who are among the most striking of Kipling's creations, and were almost certainly based on the rank and file soldiery he met on his trips in India. They are, arguably, three of the most striking characters in English literature.

He also enjoyed the sheer variety of the people of all races he met. "One met men going up and down the ladder in every shape of misery and success." [20] He describes how, as a journalist, he was offered bribes but never took one.[21] He demonstrates enormous pride when he rides into Simla side by side with war hero General Roberts who would later become a personal friend. He explored the northern borders of India up to the edge of the Himalayas, within range of Tibet, territory he would later portray in *Kim*. He had an insatiable desire for knowledge and India was especially inviting with its range of religions, peoples and races. That colour remains unchanged today. To a mere youth of seventeen it was totally exhilarating. It is hardly surprising that at such a young age and with so little adult experience, he saw the characters but not always the greater political picture.

His biographer Carrington says that he knew more about the low life of Lahore than the police. [22] As we will see, Carrington also makes the rather wild and unsubstantiated assertion that Kipling penetrated the underworld of Lahore through Freemasonry. This is an indication of how little some of his biographers understood Freemasonry and the people that Kipling met through his Lodge. As will be shown Kipling's own Lodge in Lahore included many of the most senior British administrators and Indian princes. They would hardly be included in the underworld - in fact quite the opposite. In reality the Lodge included some of the most distinguished men in the district.

It was in India, as described later, that he became a Freemason and it is the writer's view that his Masonic education was the catalyst in the development of Kipling's long-term philosophy, which he later called "the Law" and which became the benchmark from which his ideas on life developed. He continued to develop his ideas throughout his working life. This was, of course, not "law" in the strict meaning of the word but a code or set of rules for existence.

It was here also that he started to construct the notion, from the relationship between the members of the Raj and the native Indians, that the scheme of things meant that the former were bred to rule and the natives, despite their continuing advancement, were meant to be subjects. Nevertheless, this did not, for him, engender any lack of respect for the indigenous population. It is rather like the address used by Freemasons at the installation of a new Master "As some must of necessity rule and teach, others must learn to submit and obey." Kipling probably acquired this view initially from his father and didn't question it. The Lodge, when he joined, would have confirmed this approach to the relationship between the rulers and ruled. Kipling, the hero-worshipper (Cecil Rhodes was an outstanding example of his worship), would have accepted authority easily. It is also evident from his earliest Indian stories that he also understood how important honour and integrity were to an army officer, who would rather die than face dishonour.[23] These were all concepts that he would have immediately absorbed during his early years in the Lodge.

It was in 1885 that he began to write the stories which would transform his life. He later wrote "My pen took charge, and I, greatly admiring, watched it write for me far into the night." [24] Kipling repeatedly, in his autobiography, claims the existence of this almost divine force which guided his writing- his "Daemon". The collection *Plain Tales from the Hills* was published in 1888 and was the first major demonstration of his remarkable talent. Many of the forty *Tales* had appeared in the *Civil and Military Gazette* in the preceding two years. They are full of youthful exuberance. Some are irreverent, others comic or tragic. They cover almost every level of Indian life, and his Indian readers could easily recognize the type of characters that he portrayed. This was the first plank in Kipling's fame. He followed that, the next year, with *Soldiers Three*, which introduced the three rank and file soldiers, Mulvaney, Ortheris and Learoyd.[25] These stories were produced in a cheap edition that sold at railway stations for a penny, and became an almost instant success. So immediate was their popularity that in little time word of this new talent had spread to England. To English readers Kipling's stories were so unlike any they had read before, that they made an almost disproportionate impact.

After nearly five years in Lahore, Kipling was transferred to Allahabad, where in the autumn of 1887 he joined a larger newspaper *"The Pioneer"*. This was also a significant change of environment. Lahore was a mainly Muslim city, whereas Allahabad was principally Hindu. Kipling had by now realized the commercial value of his stories, and started to accumulate the funds that would enable him to leave India and try his hand in England.[26] In a matter of barely a year his reputation had spread beyond the sub-continent, and was attracting interest from publishers in England. With increasing confidence he had also risen above the level of a conventional junior newspaper reporter, and his printed opinions on topical matters were often too controversial for his editor's comfort. Within months of arriving in Allahabad he became increasingly restless, and had by now saved enough money to implement his long term plans. He was also affected by the summer heat and could not always escape to Simla or the hills rather than endure the torrid summer temperatures in the city.

He resolved to leave India, and had accumulated enough money to do that. He was only to return to India once for the briefest of visits, but India was in his blood. "For the rest of his life he would remain, to some extent, a 'returned Anglo-Indian': a homeless man who left a vital part of himself in the East; a writer whose view of the world was inexorably conditioned by the land and the people amongst whom he had grown to maturity." [27]

Kipling finally quit India in March 1889 and, in what was to become a regular habit, began the first of his many travels. He voyaged from Calcutta via Burma, Singapore, Hong Kong and Japan and finally to the United States where he criss-crossed the country before joining his friends Professor Alick Hill and his wife Edmonia, who had been his close confidante and with whom he had stayed for much of the time during his last year in India. He used the journey to write further articles for the newspaper, some of which later became the volume *From Sea to Sea*.

He completed this part of his journey in San Francisco, where his fame had preceded him. There he got a mixed reception for some of his tactless comments on American life and habits. Kipling was not always the personification of diplomacy and tact. He ventured briefly into Canada before resuming his travels in the USA and visited Yellowstone, Salt Lake City and Chicago. He spent more time with the Hills and their family and continued his trip via Washington and Boston. There he made a visit to Mark Twain, starting a friendship that would continue until Twain's death in 1910. (Coincidentally Twain was also a Freemason). After being initially critical of the

United States, he later seems to have developed a great affection for the country, which would eventually lead him back there. His relationship with the United States would undergo several dramatic changes. After all these travels his funds were depleted and he went to New York and finally in October 1889, travelling with Mrs. Hill and her sister, he departed for London.

Back in England

Kipling had not lived in England as an adult, and he arrived back at 24 years old, already famous and lionized. "It was all whirlingly outside my comprehension", he wrote of this period.[28] Yet, just as he had absorbed every aspect of life in India, he did the same in London. At times in those first days funds were low but 2d (less than 1p in modern currency) could buy him a filling supper of sausage and mash. [29] He visited the local music hall where he found inspiration for some pieces in *Barrack Room Ballads*. He was soon publishing verse and perhaps more importantly arranging publication of English editions of *Plain Tales from the Hills* and the *Indian Railway Library Stories*. He established relationships with publishers and an agent.

He found rooms in Villiers Street and Mrs. Hill and her sister Caroline Taylor helped him settle in. Soon, he started to make contacts in the literary and publishing world and he had little difficulty in finding publishers for his work. Within two months of his arrival *The Ballad of East and West* was published, although under a pseudonym. Even the elderly Poet Laureate Tennyson took notice of this new arrival as [30] that famous line was first presented to the reading public:

Oh, East is East, and West is West, and never the twain shall meet,

As many critics have appreciated, like other famous Kipling quotations, it is often misunderstood. The sentiment, if one reads the whole stanza, is that although East and West may be poles apart physically, deep down all men are the same in spirit.

1890 was his first full year in London and a hectic one. Everyone wanted to meet this young author, although he was treated as something of a curiosity. Initially it seems that Kipling was lonely and he found literary London stuffy, and alien to someone with no adult experience in England. Such was his celebrity that he even became the subject of a *Times* leader. He saw Florence again but the relationship did not revive. It did, however, lead to his first novel *The Light That Failed*, where the heroine is quite unequivocally modelled on Florence. As so often happened with Kipling, the novel distilled his personal experiences and emotions, with the addition of his own meticulous research. It seems he had a brief relationship with Edmonia Hills' sister Caroline Taylor.[31] He rapidly acquired literary acquaintances including Edmund Gosse, Rider Haggard, Thomas Hardy, Henry James and several other established authors. This was no mean achievement for a man not yet twenty-five years old. Kipling was not overawed by these famous contemporaries. He spent time with his family, including his cousins the Baldwins and Burne-Jones. But the overall impression one gets is that Kipling missed India and found London a lonely place. He was encouraged by the editor W.E.Henley who published a number of his poems that would later be put together as *Barrack Room Ballads*.

He completed *The Light That Failed* but then, after a lengthy period of sustained work, his health collapsed. This was to be a regular pattern in his literary life where he worked intensively until his health broke down. He sailed for Italy, where he stayed in Naples as a guest of Lord Dufferin, the former Governor-General of India, who was then the British Ambassador to Italy.

Then he became embroiled in a long-running dispute over his copyright, which had been pirated in the United States. American copyright laws were still in their infancy and it was relatively easy for publishers across the Atlantic to abuse the copyright of the Indian stories, many of which had previously appeared in newspapers.

The Balestiers and Marriage

It was in this period that Kipling began a close friendship with Wolcott Balestier, an American literary agent living in London, who was only four years older than Kipling. Balestier was one of four children from an established and prosperous East Coast family, and clearly the brightest member of the family. He had been sent to London by an American publisher to exploit the growing market for British writers who wanted to publish in the USA. As an English writer who had already had problems protecting his copyright in the USA, Kipling must have seemed an obvious target, as well as the fact that he was now hugely popular on both sides of the Atlantic. Wolcott's sister Caroline, who seems to have been devoted to her clever brother, later acted as hostess to the salon Walcott created in London. Balestier's visitors included Edmund Gosse and fellow American Henry James. Like Kipling, Wolcott had been a journalist and was impressed with the young Kipling who was introduced to him by Gosse.

Kipling, still in his early twenties, was attracted to the Balestiers and developed a close friendship with Wolcott. The Americans, in turn, were thrilled to have the youthful and already world famous writer among their close friends and growing salon. After they first met, early in 1890, the attraction between Rudyard and Wolcott developed almost immediately. Some biographers have speculated that Wolcott was a homosexual and that he and Kipling may have become lovers. In his later writing, Kipling wrote viciously about homosexuality, and some observers have questioned whether his almost violent reaction can be interpreted as evidence that he and Balestier indeed had a sexual relationship. There is absolutely no evidence to substantiate this. Martin Seymour Smith, in his somewhat notorious biography of Kipling which explores the issue more than most, devotes much space to an examination of Victorian sexuality and sexual repression, but still comes to the conclusion that however close Kipling and Wolcott became, it was not a physical liaison.[32] However the two young men embarked on writing a novel together, *Naulahka —A novel of East and West*, which Kipling completed and published after Balestier's death.

What is clear is that they became very intimate friends, described by Wolcott's sister Josephine as "the two young lions". A place was set for Kipling at every meal time at the Balestiers' home. Indeed, Caroline's biographer Adam Nicholson has said that if he was having an affair, Kipling's affair was with the whole Balestier family. [33]

Caroline was three years older than Rudyard. As in the relationship with Edmonia Hill, he seems to have been attracted by an older woman. Perhaps this can be related back to his experiences in India where the seductive Mrs. Hauksbee plays such a prominent role in several stories in

Plain Tales From the Hills. [34] There must have been several bored middle aged women like her, abandoned by their husbands in Simla for the summer. However, before this relationship could develop any further, Kipling decided to take a long trip. "My need was to get clean away and re-sort myself." As happened periodically throughout his life Kipling fell prey to the stresses of overwork. It was intended that the trip would include visiting Robert Louis Stevenson in Samoa. He left on the first part of the trip, which took him to Cape Town where he made his first acquaintance with Cecil Rhodes. He also met the South African novelist Olive Schreiner author of *The Story of An African Farm*. From there he travelled to New Zealand, but he never reached Samoa and Stevenson. Kipling had a great regard for Stevenson and it became a lifelong regret that they never met. In his autobiography he says of RLS, " ….I was an Eminent Past Master in RLS. Even to-day I would back myself to take seventy-five per cent marks in written or viva voce examination on *The Wrong Box* which, as the Initiated know, is the Test Volume of that Degree."[35]

He briefly travelled with "General" Booth of the Salvation Army (another Freemason). He left New Zealand and travelled to Colombo and then on to Lahore, intending to spend Christmas with his family. He had hardly arrived in India when a telegram reached him, with the news that Wolcott Balestier, on a business trip to Germany, had been taken ill with typhoid and had died in Dresden on December 6th. In less than two weeks from receipt of the news, Kipling was back in London. The day after his return he took out a special licence and married Caroline on 18th January 1892. Henry James, one of only a handful of witnesses, described it as "a dreary little wedding".[36] London was in the midst of an influenza epidemic and both Rudyard and Caroline's relatives were prevented from attending because of illness. Biographers have speculated about the haste with which the wedding was arranged and whether Kipling had made some sort of promise to Wolcott to look after his sister, or whether before his trip Kipling himself had proposed to Caroline. Why did the marriage take place so soon after his return? Neither explanation would justify the speed with which the wedding was held. Balestier gets no mention in his autobiography, but then very few of the other people close to Kipling appear in it, apart from his parents. The narrative leaps from his Indian trip to his wedding and honeymoon.

Caroline had arrived in England less than three years earlier. Her biographer describes her, in her teens, as "headstrong, unattractively interested in art and poetry, prepared to stand outside the norm."[37] Biographer Charles Carrington, describing Balestier's impact on literary London, said that he would have been forgotten, but concludes "....his personal conquest of Rudyard Kipling was an event in the history of literature." [38] It is interesting to speculate what direction Kipling's career might have gone if he had not met the Balestiers and married Caroline.

It is puzzling that, from that point onwards, any reference to Wolcott seems to have been virtually eradicated from their lives. No correspondence with him survives. It seems that, like the other losses he suffered later in life, Kipling repressed the memory. Many Kipling biographers have painted Caroline as the guard dog protecting Kipling from the outside world, and even her biography is entitled *The Hated Wife*. Although she has been described as harsh and bullying, she seems to have fulfilled a need for Kipling, and to have provided the structure to his daily life that he would not otherwise have had. She appears to have managed all aspects of their domestic lives, and ensured that he got the privacy that was so important to him.

Before departing on honeymoon Kipling published *Barrack Room Ballads*, which was an immediate best seller and was regularly reprinted. On their honeymoon trip they first visited Caroline's home at Brattleboro in Vermont. Kipling delighted in the winter scenery in New England. His relationship with Caroline's brother Beatty and his wife Mai was cordial. Caroline, however, had a strained relationship with her wild and rowdy brother, whom she regarded as grossly inferior to her late brother Wolcott, and to her world renowned author husband. The Kiplings were flush with funds and Beatty was continually broke. However, Kipling was enchanted with New England and immediately agreed to buy some land from his brother-in-law, on which to build a house. At this stage of his life Kipling was very much in love with America.

After this initial visit they continued their honeymoon, travelling to the Far East and Japan. It is evidence of Kipling's already international standing that, while in Japan, he discovered that his bank had become insolvent and he had lost all his funds. Thomas Cook advanced him the funds that he needed and he continued his trip. His financial problems were short-lived, as royalties from his books were now pouring in steadily. Nevertheless a further attempt to visit Robert Louis Stevenson in Samoa was cancelled.

The United States

The newly-weds eventually returned to Brattleboro in 1892. They rented "Bliss Cottage" there and started building a house on the piece of land that they had bought from Beatty, who was put in charge of the building works. Their first daughter, Josephine, was born on 29th December 1892. This period was a happy one for Kipling and he began writing what would become the *Jungle Books*. From the birth of Josephine his delight in children grew and he produced what are now his most durable works. Kipling could be difficult and spiky with adults but never displayed that aspect of his temperament towards children. As his fame grew during this period, an increasing number of journalists and visitors beat a path to Brattleboro, but his antipathy towards the press developed into a serious aversion. For a former journalist (he would become one again later), he had little tolerance for newspapermen and Caroline increasingly adopted the role of the dragon at the gate to protect his privacy.

During the first two years at Brattleboro, Kipling continued to be productive. Its relative isolation gave him the peace and quiet to write. It was in late 1894, during a visit by Conan Doyle, that he wrote the poem *My Mother Lodge* in a single morning. He also enjoyed an extended visit from his father, Lockwood, who undoubtedly had some input into his son's work - especially where any aspect of India was involved. He and Caroline also had time to holiday and, on a trip to London, Kipling, still not yet thirty years old, was again lionized. He was saddened by the death of Robert Louis Stevenson with whom he had corresponded for many years. In England he attended a farewell celebration for Crom Price who had retired as Headmaster of United Services College. Price was naturally proud of his celebrated former pupil.[39]

But, back in Brattleboro, a deeper problem was brewing. Caroline and her spendthrift brother Beatty quarreled. She constantly challenged how he spent the money he was given for the building work. No sum was too small to be checked. Beatty, generally an easy going character, resented his controlling sister. The new home was called Naulakha, based on the name of the book that Rudyard had co-written with Wolcott Balestier. The building was completed and the Kiplings moved into their new home, but remained largely aloof from the surrounding community. Although they made some friends, their life style and household were modelled more on the upper class English country house and the way of life he had enjoyed with his parents in India. When he wished for company, Kipling frequently escaped to Boston, leaving an embattled Caroline to deal with business and domestic issues. Throughout their married life she struggled to retain servants. Staff turnover was a continual problem. The Kiplings ran their home as if they were still in England, with liveried staff, dressing for dinner and treating the staff with a very un-American reserve. Kipling seemed to want to preserve the formality of the Raj.

One of many trips that the Kiplings made from Brattleboro was to Washington, where he was invited to the White House to meet President Cleveland. Kipling was not impressed by the Cleveland administration, which he thought represented the worst of America. On the same trip he met an up and coming young American called Theodore Roosevelt, and the two men struck up a friendship that would endure. Roosevelt, then only

37, would only six years later become the youngest ever American President, on the assassination of President McKinley. Incidentally, Roosevelt became a Freemason just a few weeks before he was inaugurated as Vice President, when he was initiated into Matinecock Lodge No. 806 at Oyster Bay, Long Island. It may seem unremarkable now, but here was Kipling, not yet thirty, mixing at the highest level with international statesmen and politicians. In that respect he has no equals in this day and age.

Kipling and the future President shared many views, and Carrington comments, "....though they rarely met again, they corresponded intermittently as friends, a cross-fertilization that was to have a notable effect upon both Kipling's philosophy and Roosevelt's political career."[40] Unlike Kipling, Roosevelt remained a regular visitor to his lodge. In an address to the Grand Lodge of Pennsylvania to mark the 150th anniversary of the raising of George Washington, Roosevelt wrote, "One of the things that so greatly attracted me to Masonry that I hailed the chance of becoming a Mason was that it really did act up to what we, as a government, are pledged to do - namely to treat each man on his merits as a man."

On the international front, Kipling was uncomfortable, as relationships between Britain and America deteriorated over the border dispute between Venezuela and British Guyana. This was also a prolific period for his writing, and Kipling had begun the work that would ultimately result in *Kim*. He also completed *Captains Courageous* (see Chapter Eight), appropriately based in New England. The latter book is a short novel and simple tale built around the New England fishing industry. The story tells of a spoilt child of a rich family who falls overboard from a liner, is rescued by a fishing boat and has to spend months working his passage until the boat returns to its home port. By the end of the trip the boy has undergone a complete transformation and is returned to his grieving parents as an upstanding young man. Kipling spent time in the New England fishing ports, researching his material to ensure its veracity.

Back in Brattleboro, the improvident Beatty was getting himself deeper in debt and, with the building work concluded, the Kiplings refused him any further financial help. Beatty was also drinking heavily. It was rumoured locally that the Kiplings had said they "carried" Beatty. The family feud was becoming public knowledge. Elsie Kipling, their second child, was born at the beginning of 1896 and by then family relationships were almost at breakdown. Caroline's attempts to control Beatty only made matters worse.

It culminated in a roadside confrontation in May 1896 between Rudyard and Beatty, when the latter accused his brother-in-law of damaging his reputation, and threatened him with violence. Kipling responded by going to his lawyer and having Beatty arrested for threatening to murder him.

Kipling found that this family dispute instantly became a cause célèbre in the US press. Journalists flocked to the small town for the story of the famous English writer's dispute with the home town boy. Beatty seemed to relish Kipling's obvious discomfort in the face of media attention. Following Kipling's complaint to the police, Beatty was charged and the matter was soon before the local court. The first hearing was adjourned, and Beatty released on bail. Beatty enjoyed entertaining the ever expanding pack of press men who descended on Brattleboro. The hearing was resumed the following week.

Kipling spent an unpleasant day in the witness box and Beatty was committed for trial at the next county court sessions.

After the first incomplete court hearing, Kipling lingered for another three months in Brattleboro, but it seems his spirit was broken. The publicity and lack of privacy had killed his previous pleasure with Brattleboro and Vermont. Before the case was heard, the Kiplings packed their belongings and fled. The idyll in New England ceased abruptly. It ended four happy and productive years in New England. Although Kipling would to return to America, he would never settle there again, and as we will see, misfortune followed him there. He never returned to Brattleboro or Naulakha.

Back in England

Returning to England at short notice, the Kipling family was homeless. Their first choice was Rock House in Torquay. This suited Caroline, who was anxious not to live under the shadow of her dominant mother-in-law, Alice Kipling. She became pregnant with their third child, John. But Devon was too remote for Rudyard. He missed Vermont and the easy access he had had to Boston and Washington, though he had the consolation of being near the sea. Through his naval friends, he was able to join them on manoeuvres which he greatly enjoyed, but he wanted to be close to the political and literary world in London, and he left Caroline frequently to travel alone to London.

It was while living in Torquay that he started writing the *Stalky* stories, based on his schooldays at Westwood Ho! That same year he became the youngest member of the Athenaeum Club and on the night of his admission he dined with Cecil Rhodes and Alfred Milner. Rhodes was also a Freemason having been initiated while studying at Oriel College, Oxford. Although he later became sceptical about Masonry, he remained a member of the Craft until his death in 1902. Rhodes never married and he was the subject of rumours of his homosexuality, although there is no evidence to substantiate that. Kipling's friendship with Rhodes would later become significant to both men, and Rhodes would even build a home for Kipling on his Groot Schuur estate in Cape Town.

The Kiplings remained in Torquay for less than a year. He found the weather horrid and his letters in this period are full of his dislike of the English climate. After a brief stay in London, the family moved, in June 1897, to Rottingdean in Sussex, where they would remain for the next five years. Rottingdean, then, was a quiet village and still relatively remote from Brighton. It was also the holiday home of the Burne-Joneses, the Baldwins and other members of his family. That year was Queen Victoria's Diamond Jubilee in which Kipling participated. After much deliberation he wrote the poem to be known as *Recessional* which appeared in *The Times*. Lauded by some but criticized by others, it was to contain one of the most controversial verses of his career.

The poem appeared at the end of the Jubilee celebrations. Although the Empire might be considered at that time to have been at its apogee, the poem hints at impending Imperial decline which would soon follow. Like many of Kipling's most controversial poems it also contains a stark warning. It starts

God of our fathers, known of old,
Lord of our far-flung battle-line,

Beneath whose awful Hand we hold
Dominion over palm and pine-
Lord God of Hosts, be with us yet,
Lest we forget - lest we forget!

After two more verses in a similar mood it then continues:

If, drunk with sight of power, we loose
Wild tongues that have not 'Ihee in awe,
Such boastings as the Gentiles use,
Or lesser breeds without the Law-
Lord God of Hosts, be with us yet,
Lest we forget - lest we forget.

This verse has attracted more argument and debate than almost any other lines that Kipling wrote. His detractors leapt on it as overt racism, but a deeper understanding of Kipling has suggested what was certainly his real intention in the reference to "lesser breeds". The Gentiles of the poem are defined by David Gilmour as "the Kaiser and his henchmen."[41] Kipling's "lesser breeds" are the Germans, the Boers and also the Russians to whom he had already taken such a strong aversion. It was also a call to humility and duty. *Recessional* praised the British and their Empire, but was also a warning against arrogance and complacency, and that British success could not be taken for granted. In poems like this Kipling slipped easily into Biblical vocabulary. It was also sung (it was written as if it was a hymn) to the tune of *Eternal Father Strong to Save* – a tune familiar to most Freemasons. The success of this poem raised Kipling to a new level in the public consciousness. One connection with the poem that would have gratified Kipling is that when a Masonic church service was held in Cape Town in 1946, to celebrate the Allies' victory in World War Two, *Recessional* was sung.

The highlight of the year for Kipling was the birth of his son John. The Kiplings remained active house hunters, but had still not yet found their ideal home. That winter Rudyard and Caroline decided to escape the British climate, and shortly after Christmas the entire family embarked for South Africa. They spent three months in Cape Town. There Kipling was reunited with Rhodes, and also with Alfred Milner who was now High Commissioner. Milner's main task was to seek some resolution with the Boers. He was respected as a highly competent administrator, in complete contrast to Rhodes who was considered a dreamer on a grand scale. At Rhodes' invitation, Kipling paid a short visit to Rhodesia. Back home in England, he relished a cruise with the Navy and the author of *Barrack Room Ballads* appeared as popular below decks as he was already with the rank and file in the army.

Despite his other extensive writings, international events were a very prominent part of Kipling's life at that time. His public pronouncements were frequent- some in verse, others in prose. Editors competed for his latest verses. He had praised Kitchener for his success at Omdurman; he had seen the failure of the Jameson raid in South Africa, and finally the outbreak of hostilities between the Americans and Cuba. Kipling watched with understandable cynicism as the Germans expanded their navy. The one positive was the resumption of warm relations between Britain and the United States. At the beginning of 1899 he published another poem in *The Times* which was to become a defining statement of the Kipling world view – *The White Man's Burden.*

Take up the White Man's burden-
Send forth the best ye breed-
Go bind your sons to exile
To serve your captives' need;
To wait in heavy harness,
On fluttered folk and wild-
Your new-caught, sullen peoples,
Half-devil and half-child.

Like several of Kipling poems it is frequently misunderstood. It was addressed to the Americans as a reaction to their annexation of the Philippines. Kipling's intention with the poem was to encourage the Americans, like the British, to take up the responsibility and burden of enlightening more backward nations [42], but the message was crudely delivered and attracted many parodies and attacks from his critics. Indeed it is normally produced to support claims of Kipling's racism. That was clearly not his intention, but it did highlight the imperial ambitions of the USA.

During 1898, Kipling continued working on a range of different projects, including *Kim*. Instead of going to South Africa again that winter, the Kiplings decided to pay a visit to America. This was an opportunity for Caroline to see her mother, and would enable Rudyard to deal with pressing publishing issues.

There tragedy awaited the Kipling family. They had crossed the Atlantic in poor weather and on arrival in New York all three children were unwell. Initially they seem to recover but a couple of weeks later Rudyard developed pneumonia, and then Josephine also deteriorated. Josephine was sent away from their hotel to Long Island, to be nursed by friends of the Kiplings. Caroline stayed to care for her husband, who by then was in so serious a condition that his life was considered to be in danger. The two younger children had whooping cough. Reporters kept vigil for nearly two weeks, as the world awaited news of the possible death of the famous writer. He was so ill that his wife hid from him, for several days, the news that Josephine had succumbed to her illness. Kipling was distraught when he finally became aware of Josephine's death, and it seems he never really recovered from the loss of his beloved daughter. When one looks in depth at his whole life, this was undoubtedly the greatest blow that ever befell him. He never returned to America after that trip.

A huge volume of condolences flooded in, while Kipling endured a long and miserable convalescence. The family stayed in America until June, when they returned to England and continued their recuperation in Scotland. Later that year *Stalky & Co* was published. It received a mixed reception. Perhaps, more importantly, the family was unhappy with their home in Rottingdean as it was no longer the private retreat it had been originally. The Kiplings had become a curiosity to day-trippers from Brighton, who could peer over their hedge from the tops of their charabancs.

The Boer War

By the end of 1899, the war in South Africa was already underway, and British troops were being shipped to the Cape under the command of Kipling's friend, now Lord Roberts. Yet again, Kipling the poet rose to the occasion and wrote *The Absent Minded Beggar*. This was published in *The Daily Mail,* and raised a quarter of a million pounds through public subscription, which was applied for the benefit of the troops. The poem was also set to music by Sir Arthur Sullivan (another Freemason). Such was his standing that an offer of a knighthood was made to the thirty-four year old Kipling, but was gracefully declined (as it would be on future occasions).

One result of his health problems in New York was that his doctors had urged him that he should avoid spending winters in England. On 20 January 1900 Kipling and Caroline left England, landing in Cape Town just two weeks later. Kipling immediately went to see Lord Roberts to discuss the war. At the Mount Nelson Hotel, he joined the journalists who were covering the war, and Roberts would later suggest that Kipling should join some of the prominent London press covering the war, to set up a newspaper for the troops. Kipling was soon involved in the war effort. He visited military hospitals, and the troops everywhere received him with acclaim as their champion. Roberts effected the relief of Kimberley, where Kipling's other friend Rhodes had been confined by the siege. Rhodes had conceived the idea of building a home for distinguished visitors on his Groot Schuur estate in the shadow of Table Mountain, and the Kiplings joined enthusiastically in this new project. They enjoyed living in South Africa and Rudyard was stimulated by his relationship with Rhodes, who became a close personal friend. Some commentators have contrasted the eloquence of Kipling with the apparent inability of Rhodes to express himself. Rhodes relied on Kipling to provide him with the words he needed, and Kipling in turn worshipped Africa's man of action.

The property that was built at Groot Schuur was called the Woolsack, and was within walking distance of Rhodes' own residence. The Kiplings used the property regularly for a number of years. It was there that the concept for the Rhodes Scholarships was developed. Kipling was to be one of the first trustees. Rhodes seems to have been one of Kipling's heroes (Milner and Jameson were idolized almost as much) and, after Rhodes' death, he transferred that hero-worship elsewhere. Rhodes may have been a great Empire builder, but Kipling describes him as "inarticulate as a school-boy of fifteen". [43] Their relationship was an enduring one, and after Rhodes' early death South Africa was never quite the same for Kipling.

So, after his arrival in South Africa, Kipling did briefly revert to being a journalist, working on the newspaper called *The Friend*, established by Lord Roberts for the benefit of the troops. Kipling was soon back in the throes of writing and sub-editing, producing both prose and poems. He was in excellent company, as Roberts had also recruited H.A.Gwynne of Reuters and Perceval Landon of *The Times*, with both of whom Kipling enjoyed a warm relationship.[44] Another famous writer/Freemason in South Africa at that time was Arthur Conan Doyle, whose name was mistakenly linked with Kipling in a Masonic context. In October 1901 the Masonic Illustrated Magazine reported 'Whilst at the seat of war (Brother Conan Doyle) attended the never-to-be-forgotten scratch Lodge at Bloemfontein in company with Brother Rudyard Kipling." This report was almost certainly incorrect, as Kipling was not in Bloemfontain on that date. It was also the case that this was not a scratch Lodge either, but actually Rising Star Lodge No. 1022 (English Constitution). When the Lodge met the following month, the brethren were unhappy that they had been described as a scratch Lodge. At another meeting the Lodge was honoured by the presence of Lord

Kitchener. The Lodge still meets at Bloemfontain. Co-incidentally, Conan Doyle had, like Kipling, spent time in Southsea where he had practiced as a doctor and he had been initiated into Freemasonry there, in Phoenix Lodge, No.257. Conan Doyle remained involved in Freemasonry periodically, but his primary interest was spiritualism.

Freemasonry in South Africa continued unabated during the Boer War. Lodge meetings were held regularly even in towns under siege like Ladysmith and Mafeking. Sir Charles Warren, who had been the first Master of Quatuor Coronati, was involved in the disastrous battle of Spion Kop.

As well as reverting to his profession and throwing himself into it enthusiastically, Kipling continued to take great interest in the welfare of the troops. He was distressed by what he saw as the lack of care for the wounded troops, who were tended in the most unhygienic conditions. In addition, while working with his editor colleagues Gwynne and Ralph, he suggested that they should form a club with a ritual similar to Freemasons.[45] His unauthorized biographer Lord Birkenhead, (dismissed from his role quite ruthlessly by Kipling's daughter Elsie), quotes at some length a form of ritual for this club that Kipling apparently wrote in his own hand. This was not the only time that he attempted to write some quasi-Masonic ritual. Birkenhead claims that Kipling "had a passion for Masonic ritual and ordered a set of gold and enamel medals with the initials of each editor in Greek capitals." This was not a short draft.

A notebook in Kipling's handwriting quoted by Birkenhead apparently came into the possession of Gwynne and begins:

Question: Halt! Who comes there?

Candidate: A man trying to join the Main body.

Question: Long delayed it has at last gone forward but what do you seek therein?

Candidate: Friends who bade me follow as soon as I was sure of my road.

And so it continues for 100 pages.

The club was called "The Friendlies" with a badge and ritual, and it continued to meet for some years. [46] Perhaps it was also the inspiration for the dining club we meet in *Fairy Kist* (see later). Kipling commissioned Tiffanys to produce a gold enameled badge with the motto *Inter Proelia prelum* which he translated as "Drinks Before Engagements". [47] This was not the only time that Kipling devised a completely original form of ritual based upon his Masonic experience, as will also be seen later.

Working on the newspaper, Kipling returned with eagerness to the skills he had learned in India. It was also at this period that Kipling attended the Battle of Karee Siding, where he came under fire. This was his first taste of real warfare. However his stay in South Africa was brief, and he was back in England by the end of April.

After his wartime experiences in South Africa, Kipling was convinced that however courageous the British fighting man might be, he was poorly trained and equipped. He felt the British did not take the profession of soldiering sufficiently seriously. He personally spent much time encouraging the establishment of rifle clubs, including his own in Sussex. Kipling, not always the most diplomatic of people, distressed a number of his previously loyal readers by suggesting that the English were more interested in sport than anything else. In the poem *The Islanders* he wrote that famous line;

With the flannelled fools at the wicket or the muddied oafs at the goals.

To a nation more interested in sport than international affairs, this was something of an affront. The idea for the poem was suggested by Lord Roberts [48] who was trying to attract support for the idea of compulsory military service and Kipling agreed with him that British security was endangered by contemporary attitudes. It is ironic that if Kipling was writing today he would probably advance the same sentiments. As was so often the case, when Kipling expressed views that were unpopular, he was nearer the mark than many people would care to admit. He did not dislike sport but simply felt that the armed forces did not receive the support and attention they deserved. If you read the entire poem it is easy to see how Kipling offended so many people but he continued to complain about the military being unprepared.

The same year also saw the completion of *Kim*, on which he had worked intermittently for several years. His father, Lockwood, with his vast knowledge of India, clearly made a major contribution to the detail

Kim was finally published at the beginning of 1901. As described later (see Chapter Five), this book, probably the finest written about India by an Englishman, is a work which reveals Kipling's deep love of India. Some critics have damned it with faint praise, by decrying the book as plotless (which even Kipling admitted). Although plot may be secondary to character, there are many books bursting with plot that fail to achieve a fraction of what *Kim* attains. To its many admirers *Kim* succeeds on several levels. It is the most vivid picture of late Victorian India, its characters stay long in the memory and, perhaps for Kipling, it is a description of the paradise of his childhood and the dramatic continent of his youth. Other critics have attacked it as simply a setting for Kipling's so–called Imperialist views, but, even among anti-colonial writers, this harsh verdict is not generally accepted. This writer would claim that it will ultimately be regarded as one of the finest pieces of fiction of its kind in the English language.

However by the end of the year Rudyard was back to South Africa. His new home at the Woolsack was nearing completion, but sadly Rhodes' health was failing. He died in March, and Kipling's verses were read over his grave in Rhodesia.[49] As Kipling left South Africa that spring, peace was negotiated and the Boer War came to an end.

Batemans

In 1902, the Kiplings finally found the home they had been seeking, and were to remain there for the rest of their lives. It was a remote house in the village of Burwash in Sussex. They had viewed it a couple of years earlier but missed the opportunity to acquire it when another interested party rented it. Their previous home at Rottingdean increasingly lacked the privacy they craved, although it was near to Aunt Georgy. Kipling was an early convert to the motor car and, despite the shortcomings of these new-fangled vehicles, the use of a car became an immediate aid to their house hunting. Although Kipling never drove, he took a great interest in the motor vehicle – as he did in other technological advances. The new British habit of taking seaside holidays and the development of public transport had further reduced their peace and quiet. Rottingdean had also been home to several family members. In contrast Batemans was set in 33 acres and cost the magnificent sum of £9300.

After they put their roots down, they bought further adjacent land to expand their estate and to increase their privacy. This was perhaps the most settled period of Kipling's life and in the peace and tranquillity of Batemans his literary output continued unabated. (Bateman's is now open to the public under the auspices of the National Trust). As they had before, the Kiplings guarded their privacy, but still welcomed many visitors from among their friends and family. Some biographers have suggested that Kipling was unsociable, but it is clear they had an almost unending succession of visitors; many were members of his enlarged family but also included prominent figures from the worlds of literature, politics and the forces.

A new project inspired by his new home, was to research early British history and one of the first results of that was *Puck of Pook's Hill*. This was followed by *Rewards and Fairies*. He divided his working time between The Woolsack in Cape Town, during the English winter and the summer at home collaborating with his father in England. Elsie and John were part of the initial inspiration for these books and like much of Kipling's writing, the stories could be read by both children and adults. *Rewards and Fairies* contained what would become possibly the most quoted verse in the English language. According to Kipling[50] the idea for *If* was taken from his acquaintance with Dr. Leander Starr Jameson (of Jameson Raid fame). Jameson had qualified as a doctor but in South Africa he came under the influence of Rhodes. He was apparently a tough and cynical operator, but with huge personal magnetism. The Raid in 1895, which he inspired, was one of the causes of the Boer War and although it was an abysmal failure, Jameson became a hero to many. He was briefly imprisoned in England but soon resumed his career in South Africa, becoming Prime Minister of the Cape Colony in 1904.

Despite the death of his friend Cecil Rhodes, Kipling continued to make his annual winter trips to South Africa for several years. Rhodes had left him the right to occupy the Woolsack for life, but a change of government at home soured his view of South Africa. In 1906 the newly elected Liberal government reversed its predecessor's policy and effectively abandoned most of the gains made by the victory in the Boer War. In South Africa, Jameson also was defeated and required to leave Groot Schuur, which had become the Prime Minister's residence. Kipling now had an Afrikaner neighbour on the estate. He must have realized that the South African idyll was coming to an end. He left the Woolsack for the last time in April 1908. He never returned there though he retained his residence rights for the rest of his life. [51] An indication of Kipling's influence in South Africa can be gauged from the fact that when the Duke of Connaught visited there in 1910, Kipling helped brief him on the country. Biographer Andrew Lycett discovered this fact in the Royal Archives at Windsor. The Duke had taken over as Grand Master of the United Grand Lodge of England in 1901, when his brother Edward Vll ascended the throne. Kipling included in his briefing details of various lodges in South Africa, although there is no evidence that he had ever visited any of them.

The run up to the First World War

In the next year or so, Kipling was heaped with academic honours. He received honorary degrees from Oxford, Cambridge and Durham. At Oxford he shared the platform with two old friends, Mark Twain and General Booth. He still refused a knighthood or any political appointments. He even rejected an opportunity to accompany the Prince of Wales to India. Caroline and Rudyard did however travel to Canada in 1907, where he made a lecture tour. In Canada he made influential friends, including Max Aitken (later Lord Beaverbrook) and Andrew Bonar Law, a future British Prime Minister. [52] Canada appears to have replaced South Africa in his affections. Masonic writer John Webb [53] quotes one of Kipling's speeches in Canada where, talking about Imperial Relations, he said "They face the five great problems- I prefer to call them the Five Points of Fellowship; Education, Immigration, Transportation, Irrigation and Administration." As so often we see in Kipling's works that the master of the memorable phrase was not averse to turning to his Masonic knowledge to assist him.

It was on his return from Canada that he was offered the Nobel Prize in Literature, the first Englishman to receive that honour. The award ceremony was rather dampened by the fact that the King of Sweden had died while the Kiplings were en route to Stockholm. Alice and Lockwood Kipling died in 1910 and 1911. Lockwood, especially, was an enormous loss to his son and the family. He had both charm and great skills, and knowledge of the arts. Lockwood had exercised a great but calming influence over his talented but sometimes irascible son. His parents had never been slow to criticize their son if they felt he overstepped the mark, but he had always taken their criticism in the right spirit, and that is something he may have missed after their deaths.

In the run–up to the First World War, Kipling was increasingly involved in right wing politics on behalf of the Tory party, and it was probably at this stage that his popularity started to decline. He was no longer perceived as the public spokesman for the armed forces, which had brought him so much acclaim during the Boer War. The years 1909-1914 were a period of rapid change and upheaval in British politics. In 1911 Kipling's Canadian friend, Bonar Law, became Leader of the Conservative Party. This was also the period of the climax of the suffragette battle and Kipling gained few female admirers with his famous verses containing the line:

The female of the species is more deadly than the male.

During this same period Kipling enthusiastically supported Baden-Powell, and became an early "Commissioner of Boy Scouts". He also spent much time with the Navy, who seemed to overtake the Army in his affections, but any aspirations for his son John to join the senior service were frustrated by John's poor eyesight, inherited from his father. John was dispatched to Wellington School in the hope that this would prepare him for the Army. Kipling at this time also got involved in the Irish problem and made an intemperate speech attacking the government, which led to criticism of him in the press. It did, however, earn him admirers in Ireland. However events at Sarajevo in 1914 changed everything.

The Great War

John Kipling, barely seventeen, applied to join the Army but his eyesight was well below the required standard and he was rejected for service. Under pressure from his son, Rudyard called in a favour from his old friend Lord Roberts and John was offered a commission in the Irish Guards. Sadly, Roberts died a few weeks later. John was still under age and needed his father's consent to enlist, which Kipling readily gave. After the initial hostilities, the war settled into the prolonged trench warfare which resulted in such massive loss of men. John was keen to get involved but was required to remain in England as he was not yet eighteen. Finally, on the day of his birthday, in August 1915, he said farewell to his parents and with his regiment he was posted to France. Only a few weeks after his posting, he was engaged in the Battle of Loos, often called "the Big Push." This was the first time the British Army used poison gas, and with limited success. The battle left 61,000 casualties with 7,766 dead including over 2,000 officers. Haigh was critical of the battle plan, as he felt that Sir John French's tactics meant that the reserves were held too far behind the main action. On 2nd October John Kipling was reported wounded and missing. For months the Kiplings retained the faint hope that John might have been taken as a prisoner and it was really only after two years had elapsed that they finally abandoned all hope that he was alive. For many years after, the grieving parents made extensive enquiries about John's fate, but his body was never discovered during their lifetimes. Ever since that conflict remains have continued to be found and in 1994 a grave, possibly that of John Kipling, was eventually identified. Carrington describes the effect on Rudyard and Caroline as "their numbing sorrow".[54]

After the War

John's death was a devastating blow. It is arguable that Kipling had never really recovered from the death of his beloved Josephine nearly twenty years earlier, but with the loss of John his burden was greatly increased. He may have blamed himself for using his influence with Lord Roberts to get John a commission, when he was no more physically suited to army life than his father. The health of both Rudyard and Caroline deteriorated and they increasingly travelled to various spas abroad for treatment. Caroline suffered from rheumatism and Kipling had constant stomach problems. Despite getting the best possible medical advice, Kipling's condition went undiagnosed for many years. It was only later that it was found that he had a duodenal ulcer. Kipling thought that he might have cancer and several of his later stories contain references or narrative elements relating to it. (see *A Madonna of the Trenches* and *The Wish House).*

In the year or so following John's death, Kipling and Caroline entertained many of John's army colleagues in the hope of finding more about his fate. They continued to stay in close touch with John's regimental colleagues, many of whom visited them at Batemans.

Two years after John's death, Kipling joined the War Graves Commission and he started writing the Masonic stories that would appear later in the volume entitled *Debits and Credits.* This was received coolly but is now regarded as one of his greatest collections of stories. He also devoted himself to writing a detailed two-volume history of John's regiment, the Irish Guards. This was a demanding task spread over several years, but it brought him into regular touch with members of his son's regiment. He became a trustee of the scholarships set up by his friend Cecil Rhodes, and advised Max Aitken (later Lord Beaverbrook) on propaganda. As a Beaverbrook biographer describes it, "Kipling no doubt enjoyed advising the dynamic young operator, while for Aitken to enjoy the confidence of the great Kipling, philosopher and voice of the Empire, must have been intoxicating."[55]

In the post-war period, he continued to be offered honours, including the Order of Merit, which he also declined. Already a long standing Francophile, he made more trips to France but now more frequently to visit the newly-built war cemeteries. In 1922 he met King George V and Queen Mary in France at the start of what would become a lasting friendship.

Just as he had suppressed his feelings after Josephine's death, so he largely did after John was lost. One of his small band of intimate friends was Sir Henry Rider Haggard, author of *She* and *King Solomon's Mines*. Haggard had also lost his only son, but as a child. They shared many opinions and views on life. After visiting Kipling in 1918 Haggard wrote, "He is one of the two men living in the world with whom I am in complete sympathy, the rest have gone.... What did we talk of - So many things it is difficult to remember them - chiefly they had to do with the fate of man. Rudyard apparently cannot make up his mind about these things. On one point, however, he is perfectly clear. I happened to remark that I thought this world was one of the hells. He replied he did not think - he was certain of it. He went on to show that it had every attribute of hell: doubt, fear, pain, struggle, bereavement, almost irresistible temptations springing from the nature with which we are clothed, physical and mental suffering etc., ending in the worst fate man can devise for man, Execution!" Haggard reminded Kipling of the great fame he had achieved but Kipling brushed this aside.[56]

Afterwards Haggard commented that he was one of very few people to whom Kipling opened his heart. "Practically he lacks intimate friends." They had briefly discussed their lost sons. "John's death had hit him very hard." On the question of whether they could find consolation in religion and God Kipling suggests that this is a transient relief –that "God does not mean we should get too near lest we should become unfitted for our work in the world."[57]

Perhaps Haggard's assessment of Kipling's lack of friends is a little harsh. The six volumes of Kipling's correspondence, so wonderfully edited by Professor Thomas Pinney, reveal a wealth of relationships which Kipling maintained throughout his life. He may have been selective in the company that he chose, and been wary of intimacy, but the long list of visitors to Batemans from both his family, professional colleagues, friends and statesmen suggests that he was not lacking in friends. His correspondence also illustrates the warmth of the man, in many different directions. One of his neighbours, Colonel Fielden, who had been an explorer and traveller, was ill and ailing and Kipling wrote him long letters from his own travels to keep the Colonel's spirits up.[58] When eventually Elsie married George Bambridge in 1924, Kipling was bereft by the gap left by the departure of his surviving child, and he wrote long, informative and affectionate letters to Elsie, which demonstrate the strength of the bond between father and daughter. Many of his letters have only been published in the last ten years, and early biographers were deprived of this warm and affectionate aspect of Kipling.

An excellent example of his long term relationships is demonstrated by his friendship with Baden- Powell. It is not clear when Kipling first met Baden-Powell, but that first acquaintance probably took place in Lahore between 1882 and 1884. They met again during the Boer War and in its aftermath. Baden-Powell (then a Colonel, later to be Lord) had become a national hero during the war, for helping make the siege of Mafeking a decisive victory in the campaign against the Boers. Among the forces that Baden–Powell used was a cadet corps of boys aged 12 to 15 who would later be the inspiration for the Scouting movement. The two men, born five years apart, had many similarities. Both were well connected; they held similar opinions. They also suffered later at the hands of their critics. Both were accused of being repressed homosexuals - again with no evidence to support that view.

During the Boer War period, Kipling was also close to the height of his renown as a national figure, for his support of the troops in South Africa. Although Kipling was not there during the Siege, he and Baden Powell met at Cecil Rhodes's home in Cape Town on several occasions, both during and after the war.

Baden Powell returned to England in 1903 and four years later he began the task of producing *Scouting for Boys*. In the first edition, which appeared in 1908, there was a précis of *Kim*. Kim's training in the novel as a young spy in the Great Game was converted into Baden Powell's *Aids to Scouting*. Just as scouting taught discipline and self-reliance, so Kim's training in the novel inculcates the same abilities. Scouting and Freemasonry have a considerable affinity and it is hardly surprising that there are several Masonic lodges constituted by former Scouts or having strong links with the Scouting movement (see later).

Kipling and King George V shared many views and a similar outlook. Both loved India. Both had travelled more than many of their contemporaries. Kipling helped the King with his broadcast Christmas messages. He continued to have contact with many leading figures of the day including Lawrence of Arabia (T.E.Lawrence), and Kipling was one of only eight people who received the first manuscript of *The Seven Pillars of Wisdom*.

Despite remaining a worldwide public figure, Kipling struggled for many years with poor health. Repeated attempts by senior consultants to diagnose his problem were unavailing. He even had all his teeth removed in 1921 on the advice of his doctor to try and relieve the constant stomach pain. After surgery in 1923, Kipling gradually recovered and resumed writing. He wrote *The Janeites* (see later). In his later stories, (and sometimes in earlier ones), Kipling could be obscure, cryptic and often highly technical. The old journalist's habit of ruthlessly paring his material down to the bone was still very much in evidence. He was capable at times of almost vicious editing of his work. But the stories themselves, although not received with the same rapture as his early ones, have over the years risen in public estimation. Some are easier to digest than others but some remain quite difficult. Too frequently his later short stories are neglected, as so much of his writing for children is more easily digested.

In the last decade of his life, his prominence meant writers had already begun compiling biographical material. Memoirs such as those by Stalky (Dunsterville) and Sir George McMunn began to appear. Kipling was distinctly uncomfortable with this level of celebrity but, despite his opposition to any form of publicity, the Kipling Society was formed and Stalky became its first president. It received no encouragement from the eponymous author. He wrote *Something of Myself*, his idiosyncratic autobiography which gives away very little of the real Kipling and ignores many of the major events in his life, especially those with tragic elements. He gives some insight into his creative processes, and in the final chapter entitled "Working Tools" he describes the actual tools of the writer's trade. The autobiography, published posthumously, gives only tantalizing glimpses of his thinking. He describes the act of writing as a physical pleasure but does not attempt to raise the art of writing above more artisan skills.[59]

By 1935, Kipling was approaching his 70th birthday. His cousin Stanley was now Prime Minister, and, although the two did not see eye to eye on current political issues, the Kiplings visited Chequers, and on occasion offered advice. When his birthday arrived, widespread tributes were paid to him, including greetings from the King. Caroline also celebrated her 73rd birthday. The Kiplings were due to travel to the South of France in January 1936 but, while staying in London, Rudyard was taken ill and rushed to the Middlesex Hospital. He died five days later, on 18th January, their 44th wedding anniversary. The Prime Minister broadcast a tribute, and while King George V was being laid to rest, his widow Queen Mary did not neglect to send a message of sympathy to Caroline.

Kipling's ashes were interred at Poets' Corner in Westminster Abbey, to rest beside Thomas Hardy and Charles Dickens.

CHAPTER TWO

FREEMASONRY IN INDIA AND KIPLING'S MASONIC CAREER AND CONNECTIONS

English Freemasonry dates officially from 1717, when the first English Grand Lodge was formed. It was followed by its establishment in India only eleven years later, in 1728, when the Grand Lodge of England authorized the constitution of an Indian Lodge. This bore the arms of the East India Company and many of its members were prominent figures in the Company. The Company was, in effect, the Government of India until the Mutiny over a century later, when Westminster assumed control of the sub-continent until eventual independence. Permission was given in London to constitute a regular Lodge at Fort William in Bengal (i.e. what later became known as Calcutta and today is called Kolkata). The Lodge appears in the Engraved Lists as No.72. In 1729 Captain Ralph Farwinter was appointed Provisional (sic) Grand Master for East India in Bengal and James Dawson as Provincial

Grand Master for the East Indies. For its first hundred years, Indian Freemasonry was largely confined to the eastern part of the sub-continent.

With hindsight there is evidence that the long term benefits that it brought to India were to counterbalance the rigid class system within the British army, and to provide a forum for Anglo Indians to meet, and later for Hindus to socialize free from the caste system. The significance of the role of Freemasonry in the lives of the military and British administrators and of the growing Indian middle class was not lost on the young Kipling.

In the early nineteenth century most Masonic activity in India was confined to the Lodges attached to individual British regiments. One of the first was the Lodge attached to the 31" Foot in about 1831 The Light of the North Lodge was constituted at Karnal in 1837 but, like many of these early Lodges, it did not survive. The military Lodges were often badly affected by the loss of men during various campaigns, or as result of their movements around the country, or sometimes by their return to England.

According to historians of Freemasonry in the Punjab,[1] it was from the 1840s that the movement expanded, especially after the Second Sikh War of 1848-9 and the conquest of the Punjab by Dalhousie. Before the outbreak of the Mutiny in 1857-8, five Lodges were formed including Kipling's own Lodge Hope and Perseverance No. 782. In the history of the District Grand Lodge of Pakistan its author, Rustum Sohrabji Sidwa,[2] was able to boast that on its centenary, the District Grand Lodge had not, during its hundred years of existence "found itself cornered or pushed into any political or religious malaise, at the instance of any member." In the hotbed of Indian and Pakistani religious and social differences, this represented a major achievement. Sadly, Freemasonry in Pakistan did not survive Partition for very long. As extreme Muslim sentiment gathered strength, it became the target of conspiracy theorists and was especially and nonsensically associated with Zionism. Just as Freemasonry had been a victim of totalitarian, fascist and communist regimes in earlier parts of the century, on this occasion it was a victim of the forces of religious intolerance and bigotry. Lahore, Kipling's first love in India, ceased to be a centre of Masonic life.

But while Pakistan had no Freemasonry, in India it continued to thrive. The current Grand Lodge of India had as its first Indian Mason, Omdat-ul-Omrah Nawab Carnatic, who was initiated in 1775. When the first Hindus were proposed there was strong opposition to them joining Freemasonry, by some of the Christian brethren, who claimed that the Hindus were not monotheists. After stiff resistance over a number of years, this complaint was eventually swept away. One individual in particular led a lengthy battle for the right of Hindus to be initiated. Prosonno Coomer Dutt, born in 1836,[3] applied in 1863 to be initiated in Calcutta. At that time the District Grand Lodge of Bengal had a bye-law that "No Mohammedan or other Asiatic shall be initiated without the previous sanction of the District Grand Master." An application for a dispensation was refused and a vote in the District Grand Lodge upheld that. Dutt then applied to the M.W. Grand Master of the United Grand Lodge of England (then the Rt. Hon Earl of Zetland). To support his application Dutt confirmed his belief in the existence of a single creator. Grand Lodge told Bengal to delete the offending bye-law, and reminded the District Grand Lodge that there was nothing to prevent someone who believed in a single deity being admitted to the Craft, although lodges retained the right to refuse an individual on other grounds. This argument went on for nine years, but Dutt persisted and eventually in 1872 he was initiated into Lodge Hope & Anchor No. 234. The following year, he became Worshipful Master, and was the first Hindu to hold that office. He went on to have a distinguished career in Freemasonry joining many Lodges and Degrees. Coincidentally the District Grand Master who rejected him was W. Bro. Hugh Sandeman who had been the first Master of Lodge Hope & Perseverance No. 782.

As the list of well-known Indians who became Masons clearly demonstrates, many of India's most distinguished native citizens valued Freemasonry, including Pandit Nehru and the Aga Khan, and all the major religions including Sikh, Muslim and Hindu embraced the Craft.[4]

In the eighteenth and nineteenth centuries, Freemasonry became increasingly popular throughout the British colonies, among both administrators and military men. "For the ordinary man as well as the imperial hero, belonging to the brotherhood was an indicator of one's identity as an empire citizen, a man who lived in, and pledged allegiance to, Britain's far reaching empire. The ever-growing network of lodges helped men (and women) as they moved across the Empire." [5]

By the time Lord Cornwallis became Governor General of India, in the 1780s, the spread of Freemasonry had "facilitated the intermingling of foreign officials in colonial outposts and trading centres."[6] There was awareness among the colonial administrators that they needed a forum for interaction between Englishmen and the growing body of educated middle-class Indians. The

Masonic lodge was ideal for that purpose. When Kipling joined his Lodge in Lahore, out of the 26 members, six were Indian including one Muslim, one Sikh and four Hindus.

When the two Grand Lodges of the Ancients and Moderns were merged in 1813 to form the United Grand Lodge of England, the Grand Master, the Duke of Sussex, had been keen that the Grand Lodge should help cement and strengthen the British Empire. One immediate result of that was that Christian references were removed from the Book of Constitutions. In 1840, the Duke ordered that Hindus and Moslems could become Freemasons. Despite this ruling, as we have seen, Hindus were still not considered to be monotheists and the Grand Master's direction was not carried out for several years. The history of Indian Freemasonry is complex and absorbing and would take more than this volume to explain, but for any Brother interested, it is well described in Robert F.Gould's magisterial six volume history.[7]

By the 1860s, Indian princes were being initiated into Freemasonry and by the time Kipling joined in 1886, Lodges were attracting a larger number of anglicized Indians. The Craft had become a meeting ground between different races and religions, as Kipling clearly recognized. The Maharajahs Duleep and Rundeer Singh were initiated into Kipling's own lodge Hope and Perseverance in Lahore in 1861.

Lieutenant General Sir George McMunn, a military man and a Freemason, writing of Freemasonry in India says," ...and everywhere in the British Empire, it is, perhaps, the greatest support that religion, morality and order have, however little we suspect it." [8] Sir George, writing before the Second World War, is one of the few Freemasons to address the link between the Craft and Kipling's writing: "The fact that it also works its secrets, its lessons and its ceremonies through a stately ritual, unwritten and handed down through the ages, at once appealed to his literary instincts, and to his ear, apt for effective phrases." Sir George also belonged to a distinguished group of District Grand Masters of Bengal (1920-1923), one of his famous predecessors being Field Marshal Earl Kitchener of Khartoum who was District Grand Master from 1903 to 1909.

When the formation of Lodge Hope and Perseverance was proposed, the site selected for it was in the Anarkali part of Lahore, away from the more predominantly white area near the Punjab Club. It was in the Punjab Club that the bachelor Kipling later spent many evenings, not always happily. According to the Lahore Chronicle[9] the new Lodge was sponsored by Jullunder Lodge. The newspaper reported "Lahore – a meeting of Free and Accepted Mason was held on Wednesday December 8 1858, to consider the advisability of opening a lodge in the Punjab, and the result has been an application to the Provincial Grand Master for a Warrant. The new Lodge will indulge in the euphonious title of Hope and Perseverance." The Freemason's Magazine [10] reported on November 5 1859 "one hundred and fifty native chiefs assembled for the ceremony (laying the foundation stone) open 6th September 1859, at which Wor. Bro. H.D.Sandeman officiated."

The Lodge met properly for the first time on St. John's Day, 27th December 1858 in Lahore. By the time that the young Kipling returned to India, some 23 years later, there were four more Lodges in Lahore comprising Fidelity Mark Lodge No.98, Mt. Ararat Ark Mariners Lodge,

Lodge Industry No. 1485 and St John the Evangelist No. 1483 meeting at the nearby army base at Mian Mir. It appears that Hope and Perseverance became the most important Lodge and its hall attracted visitors from all over the Punjab. According to Sidwa, the young Lodge sponsored the formation of Ravee Lodge No. 1215 in 1868 and the installation ceremony of Indus Lodge was also held on its premises in December 1869. To add further kudos to the Lodge, it was there that the District Grand Lodge of the Punjab was formed in March 1869 and Major Charles McWhirter was installed as the first District Grand Master. The ceremony was conducted by W.Bro.G.H.Daly, the Master of Hope and Perseverance. Later the hall became the headquarters of the District Grand Lodge. Later still, as Masonry grew in the province, the District Lodge counted about 650 members in twenty Lodges. [11] It was the custom for Lodges to combine for the installation of Masters and, in 1880, at an installation held under the banner of Hope and Perseverance, three Masters were installed. This practice later died out.

As mentioned the Lodge building for Hope and Perseverance was a distance away from the Punjab Club, where the unmarried ex-patriots met on most evenings. Kipling visited and dined there from soon after his return to India. Still a teenager, he would have been much younger than the average diner. Several of his biographers have reported Kipling's discomfort when, in the club, he was blamed for the policies of his newspaper when he was merely a junior reporter with no influence over the editorial policy. In his biography [12] he refers to the controversial issue where he was actually heckled in the club; this was over the Imbert Bill, a proposal that would have allowed

Englishmen to be tried by an Indian magistrate, which was greatly resented by the "ex-pats".

Kipling's Masonic Career

"In '85 I was made a Freemason by dispensation (Lodge of Hope and Perseverance No.782 E.C.) being under age, because the Lodge hoped for a good Secretary. They did not get him, but I helped, and got the Father to advise, in decorating the bare walls of the Masonic Hall with hangings after the prescription of Solomon's Temple. Here I met Muslims, Hindus, Sikhs, members of the Araya and Brahmo Samaj, and a Jew Tyler who was priest and butcher to his little community in the City. So yet another world opened to me which I needed."

This is Kipling's own description of his entry into Freemasonry in *Something of Myself*. [13] He was just twenty years old plus two months on his initiation. Surprisingly Kipling seems to have his date wrong. If he had been initiated in 1885, he would still have been only nineteen. He may well have been proposed for membership in 1885. The minutes of the Lodge apparently show that he was initiated on 5th April 1886.He was proposed by W.Bro. Colonel Menzies who was President of the Punjab District Board of General Purposes and his seconder was Bro. C.Brown. Colonel Menzies would later become the District Grand Master for the Punjab.

As Kipling was under 21 a special dispensation was required before he could be initiated and this was provided by the District Grand Master. The membership list of his Lodge at that time shows a mixture of military men and Indians. The building where the initiation took place was the Lahore Masonic Lodge, the very same building that is described as Jadoo Gher (Magic House) in the opening pages of *Kim*. (see Chapter 5) Kipling's occupation was described as Assistant Editor "Civil and Military Gazette". It is interesting to compare the relatively up-market membership at the time of his initiation with the brethren described in the poem *My Mother Lodge* (see Chapter 7) who are clearly fictional and bear little relationship to those in the real Lodge.

I have searched long and hard for the eventual destination of the Lodge minutes. After Freemasonry in Pakistan came to an end, little is known about what happened to Masonic materials. There is a suggestion that much was destroyed or vandalized. Extracts from the minutes of Kipling's Lodge have been quoted by a number of writers and especially by John Webb [14] who wrote that they were at Grand Lodge in London. However, a detailed search there has produced no evidence of them or at any of the other possible places and I have relied on the accuracy of those who have quoted extensively from them in other publications

What motivated Kipling to become a Freemason? In a country overshadowed by the social and cultural gap between the British and the Indians, and among the Indians themselves by religion and caste differences, Freemasonry was the only institution that made a genuine attempt at universal brotherhood. Masonry in India, both before and after the Mutiny, had grown at a steady rate. Not only did it provide a meeting place to bridge gaps between the different communities and religious groups but also some recreation for the ex-patriots. It also bridged the gap between different groups of ex-patriots - especially the military men and the civilian administrators who otherwise would have had very limited points of contact.

Here the soldiers and the civil servants, engineers and judicial officers could meet on common ground.

Kipling was certainly aware of Freemasonry long before he joined the Craft. As early as December 1882 when he was still only a few days short of his seventeenth birthday he wrote to his aunt Edith Macdonald," On Wednesday however I am going to a big Masonic Banquet where in default of my seniors I shall have to give thanks for the Press in a speech." [15] His editor had fallen off his pony and was confined to bed, leaving the teenage Kipling to run the newspaper for several days and clearly deputize at a dinner. This was almost certainly his first contact with Freemasonry.

It would certainly have been a strong attraction to Kipling who wanted to meet as wide a cross section of people as possible, and Freemasonry offered an opportunity to do that. There is no extant evidence of how he came to be proposed, other than that he was already probably quite well-known for his role as Assistant Editor of the local newspaper and he will have mixed with many of the members of his future Lodge both professionally and socially. As will be apparent from his poem *My Mother Lodge* (see later), there were not just Hindus, Moslems and at least one Jew in the Lodge, but also Anglo-Indians, both military and civil. Because of their different religions, at their festive boards some brethren did not eat, as caste or religious rules debarred them. Beef was forbidden for the Hindus and pork for the Moslems and Jews. The poem was written many years after Kipling left India and it is likely that it is more of a nostalgic recollection, than an accurate description of his Lodge, but it is still a clear indication of the wide mix of members. In the Kipling stories with a Masonic element, the members of the Lodges or the Masons that we meet are from diverse backgrounds- from the humble non-commissioned soldier in *Kim* to the most senior ranks. Like all Kipling's Masonic writing, the key constituent is always the search for universal brotherhood.

Kipling's official biographer Charles Carrington wrote, "One of the channels by which he penetrated the underworld was Freemasonry, a system which gratified both his craving for a world-religion and his devotion to the bond that unites the 'Sons of Martha', the men who bear the burden of the world's work."[16] This is fairly typical of the misinterpretation of Kipling's motivation and also a degree of ignorance by the writer. Carrington, like other later biographers, also ascribes to Kipling a depth of understanding that one would not normally expect in a young man of 20. He goes on to say "In caste-ridden India, Freemasonry was the only ground on which adherents of different religions could meet on the level". That is true, but it is quite ludicrous for him to suggest that somehow this connected Kipling to the underworld, especially as Kipling himself had already explored that in his early days in Lahore. Looking at the list of members of his Lodge it seems highly unlikely, if not laughable, that they had any underworld connections. Carrington, regarded as a reliable biographer, is wildly off target on this point. In suggesting that it satisfied his craving for a world religion, Carrington demonstrates his lack of understanding of Freemasonry and the extent it rejects any attempt to label it as a religion. Its strength, especially in India, was that it cut across religion and offered a bond between men regardless of their faith, as *My Mother Lodge* clearly shows.

Carrington, writing about Kipling's later work says, "The strongest continuing motive in his work throughout his whole career was the sense of comradeship among men who share a common allegiance because committed to a common duty."[17] He added "Freemasonry, with its cult of common action, its masculine self-sufficiency, its language of symbols, and its hierarchy of secret grades, provided him with a natural setting for his social ideals." This may have been what Kipling found once he had joined the Lodge, but in his autobiography Kipling makes it clear that he was approached to join the Craft because the Lodge needed a secretary. It is also probable that curiosity and his love of meeting new people in new environments led him to join. Like many before him Kipling became a Mason because he was encouraged by friends, colleagues or relatives but, having joined, he discovered that he had found an institution which offered a code for life, as well as a wider circle of friends and contacts. From the Lodge's point-of-view, who better than a bright young journalist to be their secretary? It was also an indication of the relative maturity of the young Kipling. As he grew and developed, the ideas he drew from Freemasonry became part of his thinking, as will be clearer when examining his philosophy. (see Chapter3) Many Kipling biographers emphasize his attraction to "in-groups" and Carrington says its secrecy and hierarchical structure appealed to him, but this does not sit comfortably with the fact that he never advanced in the craft or made more than a cursory appearance at a Lodge after he left India.

Although his father, John Lockwood Kipling, visited the Lodge premises, there is no evidence that he was ever a Freemason. He had been Professor of Architectural Sculpture at the Sir Jamsetjee Jejeebhoy School of Art. Sir

Jamsetjee, who died shortly before Kipling Senior took up his position, had been an eminent Freemason and India's first knight and baronet. He was a self-made man and renowned philanthropist, who endowed the school and many other major Indian projects.

It was only one month after his initiation that Kipling was passed to the Degree of a Fellowcraft. The Lodge did not meet during the summer, when many of its members and their families would retreat to the hills, and the cool of towns like Simla. In December the same year, he was raised to the sublime degree of a Master Mason. The minutes recording that latter ceremony were actually written by Kipling himself. Kipling's Masonic career was under way. By then the Lodge's existing Secretary had returned to England and Kipling took over his duties. Only two months later, at the Lodge's installation ceremony, in February 1887, he was invested as Secretary and carried out his duties for the next five meetings from March to July.

The Indian members of the Lodge have been identified by Sidwa. [18] They were Sirdar Bikrama Singh, a Sikh; Mohammed Hayat Khan, a Muslim Assistant Commissioner; Babu Protul Chander Chatterjee M.A., a Pleader, a Bengali Hindu; Gopal Das, another Hindu; and E.C.Jussawalla, a Parsi merchant. The latter became Worshipful Master during the time of Kipling's active involvement in the Lodge. Kipling mentions in his autobiography that one of the Hindus belonged to the Brahmo Samaj. This was a reformist movement within Hinduism. These brethren were also prominent in several other aspects of life in the Punjab. Sirdar Bikrama Singh was a member of the Punjab Jubilee Committee

Within a very short time Kipling immersed himself in Freemasonry. The Lodge minutes report that, following the installation meeting, he prepared and delivered two lectures. The first of these was given on 4 April 1887 entitled "The Origins of the Craft First Degree". Quite how a Freemason, a mere twelve months after his initiation, could research and then present a lecture that appears by its title to be quite sophisticated, is a tribute to Kipling's ability. Not only that, but he followed it in July 1887 with another lecture- this time entitled "Popular Views on Freemasonry". [19] Sadly neither lecture survives. Even for someone so comfortable with the written word, it was still a significant achievement. It was also done against the background of working very long hours in the newspaper office. There was obviously a museum and library at the Masonic hall, and it may be that his access to that goes a long way to explain the depth of knowledge he displayed in his use of Masonry in his writing throughout the rest of his life. Apart from Kipling's gift for absorbing everything he read and observed, in any era there are very few Freemasons of only a year's standing who could produce and deliver such lectures. He also represented the Lodge at Provincial meetings until August 1887. [20]

His Masonic career was further extended in April 1887 when he was advanced as a Mark Master Mason in the Mark Degree in Fidelity Mark Lodge No. 98 in Lahore, only 10 days after he had given his first lecture. On the same day he was also elevated into Mount Ararat Mark Mariners Lodge No. 98. These were the only other degrees in Masonry that Kipling joined. He never joined the Royal Arch. Mark Masonry, as will be seen, featured in Kipling's stories and poetry, although his acquaintanceship with the Mark degree was brief. Kipling grasped the concept behind the Mark degree, the pride of the craftsman in a job well done and again this formed part of his long term philosophy. Like his Craft Lodge, his Mark Lodge did not survive the partition of India and its warrant is now held by St. Martin's Lodge No.98 in Stoke-on-Trent, Staffordshire.

In the Handbook of the District Grand Lodge of the Punjab for 1888, the R.W.District Grand Master remarks that Indians were joining Freemasonry in large numbers and that it had become highly popular, "the Masonic platform has solved all difficulties; the basis of a common brotherhood striving after a higher ideal of good and the amelioration of our fellow men, has found a welcome place in the hearts of our compatriots."[21]

Apart from being Secretary, Kipling had one other vital role in the Lodge. He became the Charity Steward, in 1887. From its earliest days, Hope and Perseverance had established a fund for the children of Freemasons where the father had died. Kipling, from his reporting role on the newspaper, knew of the high level of deaths from disease among Englishmen in India. His Lodge had a fund called "The Educational Fund of Lodge Hope and Perseverance" which was the forerunner of the others that were later established. In fact when the District Grand Lodge of the Punjab wanted a fund it approached Hope and Perseverance to take over its fund, but this proposal was rejected and in 1871 the District established 'The Punjab Masonic Institution for Educating Children of Indigent Freemasons'. This was devoted solely to providing board and education for children aged six to fifteen in schools in India.[22] The Hope and Perseverance Fund was later amalgamated with the District Fund and each Lodge appointed a Charity Steward responsible for collecting his Lodge's subscriptions to the Fund. If he collected 500 rupees, then the Charity Steward was entitled to a Charity Jewel. Army regiments which had Lodges also had funds which they used to provide for children of soldiers who had died, leaving families in distressed circumstances – as we will see in *Kim*.

As will be seen from the illustration, each lodge's contribution was published, as well as the name of their Charity Steward. It appears that Kipling only took this office for one year in 1887 and by the time the report and accounts were published for the following year he would have moved on to his new position in Allahabad. He had taken this important role hardly more than a year after joining the lodge. In the accounts for both the previous and succeeding years, Kipling is shown as a donor giving 24 rupees and, by now resident in Allahabad, a further 25 rupees in 1888.

The reports of the District Grand Lodge Fund give a detailed insight into life in India in this period.[23] The children under their care are listed in the report, showing the names of their fathers, the lodges to which they belonged and the schools to which they were sent and the individual cost per child. As an example, in the 1888 report one Brother who had died left seven children, three of whom were under the care of the Masonic Institution. The Punjab District between 1886 and 1910 regularly supported between twenty and forty children at any one time, at a range of good schools, together with the maintenance of children who were too young to leave their mothers. Each yearly report identifies those children who had completed their education or returned to England. The information that Kipling would have learnt from his work as a Charity Steward is reflected in the education that Kim receives when he is discovered by his late father's regiment. (see Chapter 5) I do not think that any literary critics or biographers have recognized that the main story line in *Kim* concerning his education is derived from what Kipling learnt as a Charity Steward of his Lodge in raising funds for fatherless children.

However his busy Masonic career in Lahore was short-lived. In November of the same year he resigned as secretary and asked for a Clearance Certificate (which confirmed that he was a member in good standing and had paid all subscriptions) to enable him to join a Lodge in Allahabad, where he had transferred to edit *The World's News*. This was a larger newspaper belonging to the same proprietor and an indication of the rapid progress he had made as a journalist.

At the Lodge meeting when he confirmed his resignation, he actually recorded the minutes, including a farewell tribute to him by W.Bro J.J.Davis: "We have all heard with deep regret the intimation of our Brother Secretary that we are soon to lose his services as Secretary of the Lodge. Those of us who have watched his conduct since his initiation feel sure that he has before him a successful Masonic career for the thoroughness with which he has conducted his duties was prompted by a lively interest in his work and by a keen desire for a deeper insight into the hidden truths of Masonry. Brother Kipling has also contributed towards the welfare of the Lodge by the series of Lectures he delivered to the Brethren, which was of a nature both interesting and instructive, whilst his courteous disposition has won for him the general esteem of the Brethren. He has been all that a Secretary should be, and it is with regret that I hear that the Lodge is about to lose the services of one whom I feel sure will yet be an ornament to his Lodge and bright light in the Masonic Circle."

The minute goes on to wish Brother Kipling success in his future life and hopes that he will return occasionally to his Mother Lodge. In response, Brother Kipling thanked the Brethren for their good wishes and told the Brethren that the friendships he had formed would make a lasting impression on him. This tribute to a young man is a glowing one by any standards. In a short time he had made a very significant impact and would leave a big gap.

In a letter written to the Worshipful Master of his Mother Lodge, W.Bro. Koenig, on 22nd March 1888, he asked for his clearance certificate and for his Grand Lodge Certificate sent on when it arrived. He asked that he be treated as an absent brother. He also sent his subscription of 24 rupees and pledged any help he could give in the future. The Secretary was directed to respond to that letter.

He joined Lodge Independence with Philanthropy in Allahabad on 17th April 1888, but his active membership of that Lodge was short lived. This Lodge is now No. 2 in the Indian Constitution and was originally consecrated in 1825. It lost its original warrant when the Ganges flooded in 1837 and the Lodge's belongings were further damaged during the uprising in 1857 described in its history as "its prostration by the mutiny". It is the oldest Lodge in Upper India and only the six Lodges in Calcutta are older. [24] No information or records appear to exist concerning his brief membership of that Lodge. In its history published in 1916, it lists distinguished former members, but there is no reference to Rudyard Kipling.

He made one brief return to his Mother Lodge in Lahore the following month, when he took office and acted as stand-in for the Inner Guard. This appears to be the one and only time that Kipling was involved in the ritual of the Lodge. It was less than a year later that Kipling wrote again to say he was leaving the Province permanently and tendered his resignation. He only made one return visit to India during the rest of his life, when he stayed only with his parents before departing hastily on hearing of the death of Wolcott Balestier.

Before he left India on his travels he wrote to his friend Edmonia Hill, "I went to see a big Freemason Panjandrum who gives me a circular letter to all Lodges of America. He is District Grand Master of the Punjab." That Freemason was Edwin Woodhall Park who was a District Judge at Lahore. [25]

It was only shortly after Kipling left India in 1888, that Lodge Hope and Perseverance proposed the establishment of a Lodge for Installed Masters to be called the Albert Victor Lodge, to be named after the Prince and to mark his recent visit to the Punjab.[26]

After he left India, Kipling's life changed dramatically. He had already become an internationally recognized figure and he became increasingly more concerned to protect his privacy. He travelled extensively and despite years later finding a permanent home in Sussex, still led a rather peripatetic existence. After his involvement in Freemasonry in his last years in India, and his subsequent use of it throughout his extensive and varied writings, it is still surprising how little it impacted on his everyday life. The six volumes of his correspondence give valuable insights into his life, but surprisingly make little reference to his continuing interest in Freemasonry.[27] Kipling was a great correspondent and his letters are lively and often controversial and provide the real face that was otherwise hidden away, but only very rarely is there a reference to his Masonic connections.

Throughout his life Kipling never forgot his association with his Mother Lodge. He presented a gavel to the Lodge in 1929, said to be made of stone from the quarries in Jerusalem, and in 1935 he was made an honorary member. Eleven months after his death the lodge adopted a subsidiary title "The Kipling Lodge."

In 1939, at a meeting of his Mother Lodge, a toast list reproduced in the Kipling Journal [28] shows that for each of the ten toasts that evening, a quotation from Kipling was attached; so for example, the quotation for the toast to the District Grand Master was "Keep Ye the law, be swift in all obedience." And for Absent Brethren "But I wish that I might meet them in my Mother Lodge once more." Each quotation is completely appropriate to the respective toast.

During the remainder of his life, Kipling received invitations from many Lodges in different parts of the world. He normally acknowledged these courteously by letter, although declining to attend either for health reasons or because of his travels. I found an example of this on the internet.[29] Kipling had met an old school friend, Capt. Ernest Snow, who was visiting England from his adopted home in Canada. Kipling gave Snow a gavel that he had acquired in Jerusalem, which was apparently constructed out of four biblical woods: almond, carob, shittim and oak. The gavel ended up in the possession of Grand River Lodge No. 151 in Kitchener, Ontario, where Capt. Snow had been Master. To ascertain its provenance (apart from the silver inscription indicating that it had been presented by Kipling) the Lodge researched and found the original correspondence with Kipling to prove its authenticity. The gavel is now the Lodge's most prized possession.

Although there is no hard evidence of Kipling's attendance at Lodges (with one solitary exception) after he left India, it should be emphasized again that Kipling fiercely guarded his privacy, so it is not impossible that he did make a fleeting attendance at a Lodge meeting. One wonders whether he had any regalia and whether it is tucked away in a forgotten corner of Batemans. He did make one visit to Rosemary Lodge No. 2851, which met at the Imperial Restaurant Regent Street London on 17th November 1924. This Lodge was previously known as the Lodge of the Artists' Rifles, and still exists. It is one of a number of Lodges with military connections which nowadays are members of the Circuit of Service Lodges, which preserve fraternal contact between former servicemen. On that occasion, Kipling described himself as a member of Motherland Lodge No. 3861 of which he was an honorary member. There were over 70 military Lodges at one time but that number has shrunk as Lodges have merged, disappeared or been unable to maintain sufficient servicemen to continue their membership.

On that occasion Kipling went as a guest of W.Bro. A.S. Sutherland-Harris, who was Immediate Past Master of the Lodge and a close friend of his from Sussex. On that night, the Lodge was opened in all three degrees and part of the lectures for each of the degrees were given. Why he attended on this single occasion is hard to explain. Perhaps Caroline was reluctant to be left on her own. Like Kipling, her health was poor for the last two decades of her life.

Kipling always enjoyed the company of military and naval men. Deprived of serving in the forces through his poor eye sight, he compensated by supporting them publically and privately. He enjoyed the camaraderie of the mess and that is very similar to the ambience of a typical Masonic festive board. Even as a very young journalist, still in his late teens and early twenties, he describes how he visited Fort Lahore and the Mian Mir Cantonments and dined with them. "My first and best loved Battalion was the 2nd Fifth Fusiliers, with whom I dined in awed silence a few weeks after I came out." [30] Kipling would have been seventeen. It is probable that he visited the Lodge of St John Evangelist No 1483 there. It cannot be a coincidence that the Lodge had two members called Mulvaney and Learoyd who appear as the names of two of the characters in the *Soldiers Three* stories.[31]

Some Kipling researchers have claimed that he joined the Authors' Lodge No.3456. This is incorrect, although he wrote to the Lodge (as did Rider Haggard, Jerome K. Jerome and Sir Arthur Conan Doyle) to congratulate it on its consecration in 1910 and was later made an Honorary Member. I am grateful to the Secretary of the Authors Lodge, Bro. Ron Selby, for correcting what is a frequent mistake. Membership of the Lodge was restricted to published authors. One of the last letters he wrote on 2nd January 1936 was politely declining an invitation to the Lodge. Even then he seems to have relished using terminology so familiar to freemasons. He wrote:

"Dear Brother Spalding,
Thank you very much indeed for the Lodge invitation for the 15th, but I am sorry to say that each year I pass from the labour of fighting the

English climate to the refreshment, more or less, of the South of France, and by the 15th I ought to be there in whatever sunshine this mad world has to offer. "

He died eight days later. The Lodge was represented at Westminster Abbey for the service a few weeks later.

Perhaps his most poignant Masonic connection was as a founder member of the Lodge known as The Builders of the Silent Cities, a name chosen by Kipling. He selected the memorable words which were engraved on the gravestones, "Their name liveth for evermore."

When this Lodge was consecrated, it was attached to the Grand Loge National Française and given the number 12 in France. The War Graves Commission had its headquarters at St. Omer and the Lodge was consecrated there in 1922. Kipling was a founder member and his name appears on the warrant, but in 1925 the Commission, renamed the Imperial War Graves Commission, was transferred to London and a new Lodge consecrated in 1927 with the same name and with the number 4948. Kipling again became a founder. The French Lodge still exists under its original name, based at Lille. However, there is no evidence that Kipling attended that consecration or any subsequent meetings of either Lodge.

Kipling and Caroline continued to search for John's body for many years without success. The remains of many soldiers lost in the massive casualties of the First World War continued to be unearthed regularly for decades afterwards. Remains were eventually identified at Loos in 1994 which may belong to John and these were interred at St Mary's A.D.S., Haisnes. Even as this is written (in 2010) remains are still being found in France and Belgium.

Lodges Associated with Kipling

As we have seen, despite his relatively short active Masonic career, Kipling did join, but not attend other lodges and maintained many Masonic connections throughout his life. He also continued to use Masonic terminology and expressions. They often appear in his works as part of his literary stock in trade. Just as he often used language from the Bible, he recalled words from the Ritual that he had heard in his early twenties. During his lifetime, his links to the Craft became increasingly well-known and he was frequently invited to visit Lodges, although no evidence (other than that above) exists that he ever accepted any of those invitations. It is surprising that he remained a joiner of lodges but did not attend any meetings. It is an anomaly that a man who clearly enjoyed male company never seems to have availed himself of opportunities to attend Lodge meetings. Perhaps he was embarrassed to attend after so many years away from Lodge meetings, or had no Regalia.

Because of his association with Masonry and his international profile, a number of Lodges were founded bearing his name and most survive and thrive to this day. It is hardly remarkable that, with his interest in the Craft and the detailed knowledge that he demonstrated, he also joined Masonic Lodges of research. He was a member of Quatuor Coronati Lodge No. 2076, the premier English research Lodge, and he was a member of the Lodge's correspondence circle and remained so until his death. Quatuor Coronati was established in 1884. The 1880s were a great growth period for English Freemasonry following the appointment in the previous decade of the Prince of Wales as Grand Master.

Here we find another strong Kipling Masonic link. One of the founders of Quatuor Coronati was Sir Walter Besant, the prolific Victorian writer and a friend of Kipling. When Besant was knighted in 1895, Kipling wrote enthusiastically to congratulate him only regretting that Besant had not received a baronetcy. [32] Kipling goes on to offer suggestions for what would have been his heraldic sign. He also comments that another recipient of a knighthood, Lewis Morris, is undeserving but his proposed shield for him (illustrated by Kipling in the original letter) is an "iron, dove-tailed tenon used for lifting large stones" i.e. a Lewis! Through Besant, Kipling would have known about Sir Walter's sister-in-law, the famous Annie Besant, campaigner for women's rights, but more importantly in this context, as the founder of The International Order for Co-Masonry.

He also joined the American equivalent of Quatuor Coronati, the Philalethes Society, of which he was a founding member in 1928. Another Masonic organization that Kipling is supposed to have joined in 1909 was *Societas Rosicruciana in Anglia*, which is a purely Christian Society, open only to Master Masons. This has been claimed in a number of publications and the fact (if it is true) seems to have escaped most of his biographers. This society actively canvasses religious views among Freemasons and it may well have interested Kipling. There is no evidence that he attended any meetings.

Writing in response to a letter from Dr. Vaughan Bateson that year, and addressing him by his Rosicrucian title, " Frater" Kipling said his work wouldn't allow him to join other orders. "There's no sense in belonging to an Order unless one can attend." [33]

In his notes to Kipling's correspondence Professor Pinney comments on a letter from Kipling to his friend Sutherland-Harris. [34] Pinney refers to him as "a Masonic friend". In the letter dated 21st October 1929 Kipling says "I'll be in town on November 4 and if I can I'll come to Rosemary with great pleasure." Pinney thinks that in fact Kipling was referring to Societas Rosicruciana, but in fact as we have seen, he was referring to Rosemary Lodge No.2851. Letters to Societas Rosicruciana attempting to verify Kipling's membership went unanswered.

Thanks to the assistance of W. Bro. John Rogers, Secretary of Rosemary Lodge, I have a copy of the Minutes and Tyler's book which show Kipling as an attendee on that night. In the letter Kipling continues, "Now I send you with this promised stone I got from the Quarries of K_ S_ (sic) under where the Temple stood in Jerusalem." In fact the Kiplings had spent some time in Jerusalem in March that year. Kipling found the city fascinating, but was not particularly complimentary about it. Jerusalem in the 1920s was fairly primitive. It seems that more than one of these Kipling Masonic gavels from the Quarries may exist.

Of the existing Lodges with Kipling connections, nearest to his home at Batemans is Rudyard Kipling Lodge No. 8169, which meets at Battle in Sussex. It was founded in 1967 and its byelaws contain the sentence "The Lodge has been founded to keep alive amongst Masons the memory of Bro. Rudyard Kipling, Master Mason." [35] One of its founders was Sir Henry Wemyss Fielden, the great nephew of Kipling's neighbour and close friend, Colonel Fielden.

Sir Henry, who passed away only recently, in 2009 celebrated that rarest of Masonic milestones - 75 years in Freemasonry. On the consecration of this Lodge, corn used for the ceremony came from a farm which had once formed part of Kipling's estate at Batemans. One hundred and seventy five brethren attended the consecration and the poem *Banquet Night* was set to music and sung. The Lodge also has a special toast at the Festive Board when they drink to the memory of Bro. Kipling.

WM: Bro. J.W. , what is the next toast?

JW: To him whose name we bear.

WM: SW, who is that?

SW: Bro. Rudyard Kipling.

WM: Why do we honour him?

JW: As he honoured the Craft in his writings so do we honour him.

WM: Then let us be upstanding and drink a toast to Bro. Rudyard Kipling, Master Mason, author and Nobel Prize winner.

The Lodge also has a distinct and poetic Nine O'Clock Toast to Absent Brethren which does great credit to the Lodge and further burnishes the name of the Brother it bears.

There is also a Rudyard Kipling Lodge No. 352, consecrated in 1983 belonging to the French Grand Lodge. It meets at Frejus in the south of France in the Masonic province of Provence, and maintains the link with Kipling's great love of France. The writer, whose own Lodge is twinned with a French Lodge which he has visited many times, knows the enthusiasm and intellectual curiosity with which French Masons approach the Craft.

The Kipling family, through Rudyard's grandfather, had its roots in Northern Ireland and a Lodge exists there under the Irish constitution called Kipling Newporton Lodge No. 315. This Lodge has an interesting history. It is based in Ballinamallard, County Fermanagh, where Masonic Lodges have existed since 1767. For a long period in the nineteenth century, the Lodge fell into abeyance and the village had no active Lodge, but in 1903 a warrant surrendered by another Lodge came to Ballinamallard and a Lodge was formed.

In 1937, shortly after Kipling's death, the brethren of the Lodge decided to preserve his memory by adding his name to the Lodge's title. It was not just his fame that motivated this. Both Kipling and his cousin Prime Minister Stanley Baldwin had ancestors who came from this village. It seems Kipling was descended on his mother's side from the Rev. James McDonald who was Primitive Methodist Minister in Ballinamallard in 1784. But perhaps even more important was the fact that Kipling's political position during the Irish Home Rule Crisis had been firmly behind the Ulstermen. He had written a somewhat intemperate poem 'Ulster' which was adored by Ulstermen such as Sir Edward Carson, and which led the Attorney General to consider sedition proceedings against Kipling. [36] Kipling's views on Ulster remained controversial, and he regarded British government policy on Ireland as a betrayal of the Irish. The Lodge proudly boasts that it was the first Lodge to bear the Kipling name, beating Kipling's own Lodge Hope & Perserverance No. 782 by a month in adding the writer's name to that of the Lodge. Later the Masonic Hall in the town was named after Kipling as well.[37]

The Kipling link has spread far and wide. His daughter, Elsie Bambridge, granted permission for a Lodge in New South Wales to be named after her father. Rudyard

Kipling with Longlea Assembly No. 470 meets at Bexley, which is nine miles south west of Sydney. This Lodge was formed in 1949. In the 1940s and 1950s, Freemasonry in New South Wales expanded rapidly. According to the Lodge history, it was originally going to be called Matthew Flinders Lodge but that name was rejected by their Grand Lodge and they obtained permission from Mrs. Bambridge to name the Lodge and also to have a Lodge logo containing the elephant head that had been used on Kipling's early books.

Just how popular Kipling remains is evidenced by the fact that new Lodges are still being formed bearing his name. Rudyard Kipling Lodge No. 9681 in the Province of Lincolnshire was formed in 1998 and meets at Horncastle. Not surprisingly, it is a member of the Kindred Lodge Association, all of whose members have links to the Scouting Movement. Members of the Lodge still active in the Scout Movement attend the Lodge in uniform.

There is also a Lodge (not recognized by the United Grand Lodge of England) called the Kipling Lodge at Staines which belongs to the Royal York Rite, which claims to have its roots in Anglo -Saxon Freemasonry and to have existed since 926 AD.

After partition, Freemasonry on the Indian sub-continent was badly affected as so many of its European members moved home. Some Lodges (like millions of the population) found themselves on the wrong side of partition and either moved from Pakistan into India, or in some cases transferred back to England. Freemasonry continued in Pakistan until 1973, since when it has been banned. The District Grand Lodge of Pakistan was the successor to the District Grand Lodge of the Punjab. At its establishment in 1869 there were 217 members in the District. By 1894 the original six Lodges had grown to twenty, with 700 members, and by the end of World War One this had grown to thirty-one Lodges and 2600 members. After partition, the District was renamed and obviously had lost many Lodges and members, but by the time of its centenary in 1969 it still had twenty two Lodges and 1190 members. Sadly, after proudly celebrating its centenary, after another four years it ceased to exist.

In the history of the District produced for the centenary[38] there is no mention of Kipling as an individual member, but the printed programme contains the poem *My Mother Lodge* and another less well-known poem by Kipling, *When Earth's Last Picture is Painted,* which is a poem lauding the way that artists feel when they work for the delight of it, and finishes with the verse:

And only the Master shall praise us, and only the Master shall blame;
And no one shall work for money, and no one shall work for fame;
But each for the joy of the working, and each in his separate star,
Shall draw the thing as he sees it for the God of Things as they are!

There is nothing inconsistent with Freemasonry in this poem, but equally it was a strange choice when there are so many other Masonic poems by Kipling that could have been selected.

Freemasonry in India has continued to flourish. The Lodge in Allahabad of which Kipling was briefly a member, Independence with Philanthropy, is now numbered 2 in the Indian Grand Lodge.

Kipling was also made a member of Canongate Kilwinning Lodge No. 2 (Scottish Constitution) in Edinburgh in 1899 and from 1905 to 1908 was appointed their Poet Laureate, an office once held by Robert Burns, but there is no evidence that he ever visited it.

On the non-Masonic front, although Kipling refused many honours he did accept the offer of being an Honorary Member of the Master Mariners Company which was a new livery company in London, formed in 1927. One wonders whether that had a small resonance with the Royal Ark Mariners Lodge he had joined as a young man in India.

Evidence of Kipling's attachment to the Craft can be seen in a letter he wrote to his nephew Oliver Baldwin who had obviously told his uncle that he was about to be initiated. Kipling, saying that he was glad that Oliver was to join the Craft, wrote, "It ought to be rather a revelation to you and should increase your already not small knowledge of human nature."[39]

We can give the last word on Rudyard Kipling as a Mason to Lord Ampthill, who was Pro Grand Master from 1908-1935.[40] Proposing his toast at the Annual Meeting of the Kipling Society in 1934 he said of Kipling. "I have gone to his works for advice, guidance and instruction, and no other writer has influenced my thoughts on all things I care about, as much as Rudyard Kipling and the things I care about, apart from God and Religion, are England, the British Empire, the British Soldier and Freemasonry. In all those spheres, I admit with gratitude that I owe a great deal of the thoughts that help and guide me, to his writings."

CHAPTER THREE
KIPLING'S PHILOSOPHY

If you read a selection of the many biographies written about Kipling, you will encounter an extensive variety of opinions about the man and his work. At one extreme, to his harshest critics, he is the ultimate imperialist, a racist, a bigot and even a suppressed homosexual. To others he is the most authoritative social historian of India under the Raj, a man in touch with the people, and an astute political analyst. For some he is a veritable Cassandra who predicted two World Wars. To some literary critics he was a genius, yet others dismiss his work as limited and derivative. Controversy is never far away. Kipling divides writers and critics almost more than any other major writer in the last one hundred and fifty years. Neither his work, nor his views on many subjects, fit into a conventional pigeon hole. He was a man with many strong convictions who made no attempt to conceal his beliefs and he was quite prepared to swim against the tide of popular opinion. He did not hide his contempt for liberals. As he became older his political stance became increasingly right wing, but it did not prevent him seeing the dangers posed by the growth in Fascism in the last few years of his life.

We must recognize that his writing is far from consistent. He was not the most diplomatic of people and if living today he would not have much truck with political correctness. His political views attracted prominent enemies. With his huge output, it is hardly surprising that he could write badly on occasions, and he could be intemperate and hasty with his judgements. But he was also far more complex than many commentators gave him credit for. Although he could be irascible or given to rash judgements, yet to his friends he was a man of great warmth.

At the time of his death Kipling's reputation had been in decline for many years, although the public continued to buy his books. He was viewed by many readers and critics as an historical figure with little contemporary relevance. With the upheavals that tore Europe to pieces in the nine years after his death, it took time for literary critics to return to a more objective examination of his work and it was not until the late 1940s that serious re-evaluation began to assess Kipling's place in the pantheon of leading British authors.

Since the Second World War, the Kipling biography business has rarely slowed down. Yet despite all these analyses of his life and character, he remains a hard man to pin down. He and Caroline Kipling destroyed much of his private correspondence, and during his lifetime he declined almost all opportunities for interviews or any attempt to get him to offer a deconstruction of his work. Devoted to his friends and family, he could be spiky with strangers and especially those he perceived as intruders. One very apt description was "a man of permanent contradictions".[1] His posthumous autobiography *Something of Myself* subtitled *For My Friends Known and Unknown* is elusive, highly selective and sometimes almost deliberately whimsical or cryptic. It makes virtually no reference to many of the major events in his life, including the death of Wolcott Balestier or the deaths of his two children Josephine and John. Even his marriage is only mentioned in passing. Yet the book itself is very readable and removes some, if only some, of the mystery.

A better guide to the real Kipling may be to read his correspondence. Although much of it was destroyed, many of the recipients of his letters preserved them and Professor Pinney's masterful six-volume edition of the letters and his helpful footnotes give a much greater insight into the man. [2] These letters demonstrate not just his warmth and affection towards friends and family but also that he had a deeply caring side to his nature. They also reveal his sense of humour and a frankness that he could not always display publically. His letters to Elsie after her marriage, when he clearly missed the presence of his last surviving child, say more about the man than a dozen biographers.

The first step one should take in examining his attitude to life, in the philosophical sense, is to separate the political animal from the literary and philosophical one. Kipling's political views were often forcefully stated. He had access to most of the leading politicians of the day and was not slow to tell them where they went wrong, but his political perspective is hardly relevant here. The subtleties and nuances of politics often escaped him and it is only mentioned here to separate his public pronouncements from his profound and deep views on life and man's relationship to the world around him. It is those philosophical views that connect him to Freemasonry.

The second aspect to explore is where and how his genius was derived. He had a very basic education for a man of letters and his childhood and youth were an eclectic mixture of good and bad experiences. In his autobiography he does explain, a little enigmatically, how his stories were inspired. He calls it his "Daemon". Like much else that is personal to Kipling, it is very cryptic. It may be another word for inspiration, but the way he introduces it in his autobiography is as a supernatural spirit which takes charge of his pen. He explains how his Daemon is with him when he writes and has to be treated with care. "When your Daemon is in charge, do not try to think consciously. Drift wait and Obey." [3]

More notably, in *Something of Myself*, Kipling describes how he prepared his work and how he used his skill to prune and pare. He makes it seem that his best writing was almost unconscious. [4]

He also resented the fact that many critics looked beyond the text. [5] Kipling felt that a writer should be judged entirely by his written word and that his private life and background was irrelevant to that. He would have greatly approved the school of literary critics led by F.R.Leavis at Cambridge in the 1930s, who advocated that the text should be studied in isolation, and that a writer's life should be totally ignored when examining his work. [6] This is a difficult task with Kipling as so much of his work is an extension of his personal experiences.

Kipling would almost certainly be aghast at the seemingly endless number of attempts made to analyse his life and personality. Nearly seventy five years after his death, new biographies regularly appear, trying to get to the essence of this man and unlock his inner workings, which have seemingly eluded other writers. Although many of these opinions are reflected in different parts of this book, this volume will attempt to relate those varying views in relation to Kipling's lifelong interest in Freemasonry and how his views on many subjects are either connected to Freemasonry or originate from concepts he encountered in the Craft. Kipling's membership of Masonic study circles and approach to Societas Rosicruciana suggest that he never ceased his interest in the more profound aspects of Freemasonry. Over his long literary and public career he formulated views on life, religion and man's place in society. As one analyses these views one can see how Masonry forms a link between many of them. Kipling, from his youth in India until his last few years, never ceased to try and develop either a philosophy for life or some rationale by which man could come to terms with the adversities and uncertainties of his existence. It is evident that the loss of Josephine as a child and John in the First World War caused him to devote ever more time to finding a way to reconcile these tragedies, and this quest brings into his work many of the fundamentals of Freemasonry, which increasingly he adopted.

Kipling and Religion

One significant key to understanding Kipling's relationship with Freemasonry is to look at his links to religion during his lifetime. Despite the Kipling family's strong ties to Methodism, neither Kipling nor his father ever seem to have engaged in its practice, although his Uncle Fred Macdonald remained a leading member of the Methodist Church. Although baptized in the Church of England, Kipling does not seem to have had any active involvement in it. Father and son appear to have been anxious to avoid any formal religious involvement. Perhaps this was due to their exposure to Indian religions.

Although some biographers and literary critics have dismissed his interest in Masonry as just an esoteric pastime or hobby, others think he was attracted to Masonry in India because of its multi – racial character or simply that Kipling liked to be a member of closed societies. Another group of critics thinks he liked its quasi-religious nature. Although, he never demonstrated much interest in participation in organized religion, it did not stop him being absorbed in the search for spiritual significance and order in the universe, a quest he pursued for nearly all his adult life. Gilmour thinks that Kipling's parents had vigorously rejected their Methodist heritage and that Kipling was never a practicing Christian.[7] As we have seen, he may have joined Societas Rosicruciana in 1908, although there is no evidence of his involvement in that order. This may be just another Kipling contradiction, but more probably it was just part of Kipling's spiritual search. In fact Gilmour, in a footnote, quotes Kipling (in that same year) as describing himself as 'a god-fearing Christian atheist.' His conversations with Rider Haggard, related elsewhere in this book, seem closer to defining Kipling's views.

He had read the Bible diligently as a child (often as a punishment at Southsea), and his work is sprinkled regularly with biblical references. He would seem to relish the language that he found in the King James Bible. He was brought up in a Muslim city and many of his early contacts as a child and as a young journalist were with Muslims. There is little doubt that his sympathies in the main lay with Islam and his Muslim characters generally reflect that. He also quotes frequently from the Koran. It is interesting to speculate how Kipling would have reacted to 21st Century Muslim fundamentalism and the current clash of civilizations. It is suggested by some writers that Kipling respected the Islamic emphasis on discipline, and found Hinduism too intricate for his liking - something he may have picked up from his father, as Lockwood was equally unsympathetic to the Hindus. However, Rudyard's views did not prevent him admiring Buddhism, as is amply shown in *Kim*.

His major experience of Hindus was when he was transferred from Lahore to Allahabad, which was a predominantly Hindu city. His attitude to Hinduism was at times distinctly negative. It seems he disliked its multiplicity of gods and complex rituals. On the contrary he appeared to approve of Buddhism and the Tishoo Lama in *Kim* might even be Kipling's alter ego. The Lama's search in many ways parallels Kipling's own spiritual journey. With Judaism his relationship was inconsistent and complex. He is often understandably labeled as a vehement anti-Semite and some of his references to Jews would be unprintable today, yet there is also evidence to the contrary. Anti-Semitism was deeply embedded in English literature and Kipling would have absorbed that tradition. He writes affectionately about the Jewish Tyler in his poem *My Mother Lodge* but he makes repugnant remarks about Jews in his poems and autobiography. It is argued by some critics that Kipling's anti-Semitism is representative of upper middle class social attitudes in the first part of the century. That is a very empty and facile justification. However, as evidence that it was not an entrenched view, he enjoyed an affable correspondence with the writer Israel Zangwill, author of *Children of the Ghetto,* and the leading British proponent of Zionism. See more on this topic in Chapter 8.[8]

Kipling's Law

These different religious philosophies were all absorbed by Kipling in his youth. He developed his own concept of what for him was almost a quasi-religion, which he frequently referred to as "the Law". It was not a judicial or legal system, but the rules by which he considered life should be governed. It is part philosophy, part quasi-religion, part morality and part authority, but the moral element dovetails with much of Masonic philosophy. His reference to" the Law" is not consistent and varies according to the context, but it contains elements of the obligations that every new candidate for Freemasonry accepts on his initiation. Both Kipling's "Law" and the precepts of Freemasonry require a large measure of conformity. When he was initiated as a Freemason he would have been told to adopt "such a prudent and well-regulated course of discipline as may best conduce to your corporeal and mental faculties in their fullest energy, thereby enabling you to exert those talents whereby God has blessed you...."[9] Those words would not have been lost on Kipling. The charge after initiation also reflects much of Kipling's thinking on the relationship of man to society.

A number of leading literary figures have addressed Kipling's code and rules, without, it appears, understanding how close they are to the Masonic precepts. Simple reference to a book of Masonic ritual would have demonstrated how close Kipling's ideas are to those promulgated by Freemasonry. There are many points at which Kipling' Law and those precepts converge- pride in one's work, honour, obedience to one's superiors and responsibility to one's inferiors.

The best and most thorough examination of Kipling's "Law" may have been made by Indian academic, Shamsul Islam.[10] In his book he defined Kipling's law as "consisting of such universal values as discipline, devotion to work, positive action, suffering and love ...." Islam reviews Kipling's attitude to each major religion and, stretching his argument a little too far, includes Freemasonry as a category in his chapter, following on from the different religions. While the accuracy of his assessment of Kipling's views on each religion may be compelling, he still fails to notice that Freemasonry (which clearly makes no claims to be a religion) was the only institution where Kipling had, even in a limited sense, actively participated and the extent of its impact on him. Again this categorization demonstrates that even the most competent academics do not grasp the scope of Freemasonry and that its ability to cut across the religious divide.

Islam, in his analysis, looking at the whole range of Kipling's work, considers his Law has three ingredients-moral values, the Imperial Idea and the doctrine of disinterested suffering and positive action. [11] It is this writer's view that, towards the latter part of his life Kipling, burdened with the losses of his two children, saw the universe increasingly as a grim and relentless place (perhaps he was also influenced by his friend Thomas Hardy). Rather than submit to these dark thoughts, he sought through his concept of the Law and Freemasonry to find some escape from this void in his life. Islam, who has probably interpreted this aspect of Kipling better than many, says, "Freemasonry confirmed his faith in a universal moral order as well as the brotherhood of mankind." [12] It is also implicit in Kipling's concept of "Law" that the failure to do one's duty is to be feared more than pain or death.[13] If one examines this philosophy, it falls totally within Masonic ritual, from the obligations, charges and addresses made to a candidate during the course of the three craft ceremonies. In contrast Islam's overall conclusion is that the moral basis of Kipling's Law is directly related to the moral codes of the diverse religions to which he was exposed.[14] He emphasizes that in Kipling's world the man of action is the key person and this is reflected in so many of his works.

As has been seen, central to Kipling's world view was the importance of work. Whether he had developed this judgement during his time in India, seeing the work done by the British administrators and military, or whether it came later in his growth as a writer, there is no doubt that work as an essential element in every man's relationship with society became pivotal to Kipling's thinking. As a number of writers have realized, he may well have derived this aspect of his philosophy from Freemasonry.

This might be a convenient point to deal with the constant allegation made against Kipling that he was an unrepentant Imperialist. Most modern critics now accept that this view is greatly exaggerated. Kipling saw the Empire as a force for good and for providing order, but he also required from those Imperial administrators and soldiers a selfless dedication to their task, especially in India. In his biography, Carrington expressed the Kipling world view with great clarity, "No man had done more than Kipling to stimulate interest in the opening up of the new world, in the east and the south. He never doubted the validity of western civilization, never lapsed into sentiment over the supposed virtues of savages; but it was the spread of law, literacy, communications, useful arts that he applauded, not the enlargement of frontiers."[15]

CHAPTER FOUR

THE EARLY STORIES

By 1886, Kipling had already worked as a journalist for three years on the *Civil and Military Gazette* in Lahore. He had completed and published many of the short stories and poems upon which the foundations of his fame would be laid. His early tales had been offered in the newspaper and then printed as a collection in Calcutta in 1888 as *Plain Tales from the Hills*. They were aimed at an Anglo-Indian readership and provided a vivid picture of both the ex-patriots and the natives. His Indian audience was enthusiastic. The characters portrayed by Kipling were instantly recognizable. Kipling, at this period, seemed to soak up his experiences like a sponge. He wrote about every level of Anglo-Indian society, having had the opportunity through family and professional connections to mix at the highest levels of the Raj, but he also knew the back streets and alleys of Lahore and the Indians who inhabited those areas. He absorbed every detail of life around him. The early stories sparkle with the excitement of youth but they also demonstrate Kipling's remarkable precocity. Even after more than a century those early stories are still fresh and vibrant.

At times he is respectful of the Raj, but at other times fiercely cynical about the brutal effects of life in India. In his work in this period he seems equally at home with the colonial administrators as with the indigenous peoples. He describes a world that has long since vanished, but he delineates the images of the period in a unique way. No other writer comes close to Kipling in describing 1880s India. It is not surprising that many consider him England's greatest short story writer. These early stories mixed tragedy and comedy and later he used his ear for dialect to add stories with broad cockney and Irish accents. Because of the restrictions on space in the newspaper he was constrained to keep his stories concise and his style always reflected the need to keep his stories lean and trim, a habit he never lost.

In the same year A.H.Wheeler & Co published in their *Indian Railway Library* series the first of several volumes of Kipling stories. These were sold on railway stations for one rupee - the fifteenth part of a pound, and were amongst the early paperbacks. From the time of his initiation, Masonic references and terminology start to appear in his stories.

The Rout of the White Hussars

Some of Kipling's earliest stories, produced hurriedly for a newspaper, are often formulaic but the characters were a revelation to his first Indian readers who instantly recognized and often identified with the characters he portrayed. They also made an impact on readers at home in England but for different reasons; they had a freshness and novelty and also contained a picture of life in the

Empire that was totally new to them. Frequently Kipling's stories contain variants of the practical joke and his very first use of Freemasonry in his writings is in one such story. One can see that Kipling was having fun with his Masonry in *The Rout of the White Hussars,* one of the stories in *Plain Tales from the Hills.* This is the first Masonic reference in his writing.

The story starts with the newly-appointed colonel of a proud cavalry regiment who has angered his officers and troops, almost to the point of mutiny, by deciding to replace the regiment's much-loved drum-horse. He won't even allow his officers to purchase the poor horse at auction, although one subaltern does actually purchase it, but tells the colonel he has only done that so that he can shoot the horse to save it from mistreatment. Plans are announced to shoot the horse and to give the animal a dignified funeral. A body is carried under sacking for burial and interred with great reverence.

The following day the colonel, to teach his disaffected troops a lesson, gives an order demanding the regiment undertake tough military exercises. After these exercises, as the exhausted men are watering their horses, in the distance appears the vision of the dead drum-horse complete with kettle drums and on his back a skeleton as its rider. Men and horses panic at the sight. The Colonel, enjoying a drink in the Mess after the exercises, sees his regiment scattering and suspects either drunkenness or rebellion. The Regimental Band breaks up and runs before the drum-horse and the skeleton. The Colonel rages and drags the skeleton off the horse and it is removed by the Band Sergeant. The Colonel threatens to court martial the whole regiment but his second in command persuades him to keep the affair quiet for the sake of the regiment's reputation. A few days later the Colonel is persuaded to allow the drum-horse to be restored to his rightful position.

The final joke and twist to the story is that, two days after that, the subaltern at the centre of the conspiracy to save the horse receives a letter from someone who signs himself Secretary, Charity and Zeal, No.3709, E.C. asking for the return of their skeleton. The Band-Sergeant admits he has the skeleton which he has obviously purloined and that there is also a coffin with it. Thus Kipling creates his first fictional lodge. To his Anglo-Indian readership this reference was easily understood.

Among the other early references to Freemasonry is some of the dialogue in *Soldiers Three*. (see later in this Chapter). Kipling's early stories often contained these lighter comic elements although as we will see, the later stories, while still with flashes of humour, became darker.

The Man who would be King

This story was part of a collection called *The Phantom Rickshaw and Other Tales* and was written by the 23 year-old Kipling in 1888 while he was working as a journalist in India and was actively involved in his Lodge. In his biography of Kipling, Lord Birkenhead quotes H.G.Wells as describing it as one of the finest stories in the world.[1] Professor Tomkins thinks it a good yarn and combines Kipling's interest in what was happening on the North West Frontier with "his strong recent interest in Masonry.[2] The story is preceded by the epigraph "Brother to a prince and Fellow to a Beggar if he be found worthy." The year of its creation was a prolific one for Kipling as he probably wrote seventeen stories in that calendar year.

The origins of the story can be found in Kipling's correspondence. In a lengthy letter to his cousin, Margaret Burne–Jones, covering the period January to March 1888, he describes how he was off on a trip to Calcutta and that he was going to a big meeting of the local Masonic Lodge.[3] (If he did attend a lodge in Calcutta no record has ever been produced to confirm it.) "Curious to think that though I have come south 980 miles I am certain tomorrow of finding men who will talk to me as though they had known me all their lives on subjects on which both I and they will be able to discourse about with freedom and *camaraderie*."

He goes on to relate to his cousin an experience he had had the previous month on a train on the other side of India. He describes how he met a man who was also a Mason. "'Ships upon the sea' are nothing compared to our meetings in India." The man told Kipling that he had a friend coming across the Empire by train from the East, but he could not meet him but that Kipling's route meant his train, if on time, would cross this man's route. He asked Kipling to take a message which he would not write, to give to this man. The message was unintelligible to Kipling. "My brother gave me this message...." continues Kipling. He goes on to describe how at 5.00 a.m. on a cold winter's morning the Calcutta train drew up alongside his and he sleepily put his head out of the window.

Kipling relates," I didn't want to go threshing all down the train - there were three Englishmen on it - in my search for the unknown, so I went towards the window and behold, it was the man I was told to find; for he also (doesn't this sound mad?) was a brother of mine." The man thanked Kipling and said he knew what the message meant. Kipling comments that he didn't know the name of the man who gave him the message or the man who received it. The description in this letter confirms the great enthusiasm that Kipling felt for Freemasonry and the concept of universal brotherhood. It also demonstrates the contemporary significance of Masonry among its adherents in British India at that time.

Thus was that great adventure story, *The Man Who Would be King,* born from Kipling's experiences as a journalist travelling across India. Few biographers of Kipling seem to have picked up the source of the story from his correspondence.[4] From the brief description of this incident, it is almost certain that these men were former soldiers. Kipling makes no comment on that in his letter. There were many British soldiers who had either deserted from the army, or remained after their service finished and went fortune-hunting in India. Some, like Kim's father, Private O'Hara, succumbed to opium or drink. Others were just lazy ne'er-do-wells or, as Kipling describes them in this story, "loafers." The leading characters in this story would probably fit that label, except their ambitions were much loftier. Many of these men had been discharged from the army for breaches of military discipline, mostly brought on by drunkenness, or boredom, or the heat. Mulvaney, Learoyd and Otheris in *Soldiers Three* are fundamentally good soldiers but only when they were sober and kept occupied. The stories that Kipling wrote about them illustrate vividly the highs and lows of military life in 1880s India. As soon as they are left idle they get up to some mischief.

Kipling had met men of all ranks during the course of his working and social life. Some of his contemporaries describe him as a man ceaselessly extracting information about experiences of life and battle from the servicemen he met. The detail that Kipling accumulated and used in his stories was because his research was so thorough. [5] Where he departed significantly from most other writers about military life was his level of interest and sympathy for the ordinary soldier. It was not a sentimental attachment but a starkly realistic one, as he appreciated the very real hardships that these men underwent. Both in India and later in South Africa during the Boer War, he was shocked at the conditions that the forces had to endure.

Kipling as a newspaperman was well aware of international politics and the relationship of the Raj with its immediate neighbours. The ongoing tensions on the borders of Northern India had a massive resonance for Kipling's contemporaries, just as it should have a similar resonance for us today, as the Western powers struggle in Afghanistan. In Kipling's time the mountainous terrain separating that part of India from Afghanistan was the battleground for a war of nerves between the Great Powers. The Great Game (which also served as a background for *Kim*) was played out between the Russians and the British who were keen to curb the risk of Russian incursions into India, over those often inaccessible passes like the Khyber Pass. [6]

Another contributor to the sources of this story may well have been the larger than life adventures of the American, Josiah Harlan, who travelled to Afghanistan in the 1830s and became heavily involved in the intrigues between the local rulers, briefly becoming a Prince and army commander.[7] He travelled this dangerous country, often in disguise but unlike Daniel Dravot, survived to tell the tale. One of Harlan's contemporaries, the Englishman Alexander Burnes, like Dravot attracted to the local beauties, also suffered a horrible death at the hands of the natives.

Kipling, as well informed as anyone, would have known of these adventures and would also have been aware of the mission to Kafiristan by Colonel Lockhart. Kafiristan was at the boundaries of India and Afghanistan and had only recently been visited in 1883 by British government surveyors led by Captain William McNair who had travelled at great risk in disguise to survey this remote and hostile country. It was unknown and inaccessible. This is the country that the heroes of the story, Peachey Carnehan and Daniel Dravot, determine to conquer. It is a "Boys Own" adventure story written for adults and the young Kipling at his most brilliant. Who would expect two down-at-heel ex-soldiers to become rulers of a mountainous country inhabited by hostile tribes? But as Kipling's imagination runs riot they do it with the help of their basic knowledge of Masonic ritual. He used the encounter on the train, described in his letter to Margaret, to create a story imagining what those two former soldiers might do. The two men are outsiders; probably despised by the Indians and rejected by their British compatriots. It was only their link with Freemasonry that kept them vaguely respectable.

This story is adored by some. Professor Tompkins also enthused, "All the finer points of conception and craftsman could be missed, and the incandescent imagination, the blazing excitement, the manly pathos of it would still be entirely accessible and commanding."[8] At the other end of the spectrum, a somewhat curmudgeonly Kingsley Amis's verdict was "the grossly overrated long tale."[9] This is an opinion that is very much in a minority. This longer story was certainly a departure from the very concise short stories that had appeared in the newspaper. Those newspaper stories were "turn-overs", i.e. they started on one page and were concluded on another.

The narrator of the story is a young journalist, and if not modelled on Kipling himself, must bear many similarities to the young, hardworking and overstretched newspaper reporter travelling around India. The vivid description of the newspaper office where the narrator works fits very comfortably with Kipling's own picture of it in his autobiography. The narrator starts by bemoaning the fact that he is on a tight budget, and is therefore travelling on the Indian Railways in Intermediate class, which ranks below first and second, has no cushions and is rarely used by Europeans. During a stop on the journey he is joined by another European, whom he identifies as "a loafer", who relates his adventures but is clearly down on his luck. He asks the narrator his future plans and begs him to alter his return journey so that he can look out for a man at a certain junction that he will pass and give him a message. "I ask you as a stranger-going to the West."[10]

The journalist replies, "Where have *you* come from?"

"From the East", is the reply, "and I am hoping that you will give him a message on the Square- for the sake of my Mother as well as your own."

Kipling does not hesitate to take the wording from the third degree ceremony. To a modern day Mason, this would be an immediate signal that he was talking to a Freemason, but Kipling, to assist the reader, continues,

"Englishmen are not usually softened by appeals to the memory of their mothers, but for certain reasons, which will become fully apparent, I saw fit to agree." The narrator promises to do his best to deliver the message. During the conversation he realizes that the man has plans to impersonate a journalist in order to blackmail a local Rajah

In the film of *The Man Who Would Be King*, directed by John Huston, the narrator is specifically identified as Kipling. The narration of the story in both book and film starts with the train journey and finishes in the newspaper office, resembling the office where Kipling worked. Describing his working life in Lahore he said "I never worked less than ten hours and seldom more than fifteen per diem." He continued, "Yet I discovered that a man can work with a temperature of 104, even though next day he has to ask the office who wrote the article." As an indication of the hard life and heavy workload he added, "Death was always our near companion."[11]

Some days later, the narrator, on his return journey, stops at the junction and finds, in a second class carriage, the man who had been described to him, and conveys the cryptic message he had been asked to pass on. As he assesses the two men he has met, he realizes that they are bound on criminality and he reports them to the authorities, expecting that they will be deported.[12]

In a brief descriptive passage Kipling paints the most vivid picture of life in an Indian newspaper office and in some ways every daily newspaper office the world over. The story resumes at 3.00 a.m. on a viciously hot Indian night as the narrator/Kipling is putting the newspaper to bed, when suddenly the two men he had met on his train journeys appear in his office. He is more interested in going home and getting some sleep than talking to these "loafers".[13]

Frightened that they have come to revenge themselves for his action in reporting their plans to the authorities, the alarmed narrator is relieved to be told that they want advice, not money. They are aware that he had informed on them to the authorities and want a favour in return for overlooking that. They then introduce themselves as 'Brother Peachey Carnehan' and 'Brother Daniel Dravot'. They claim to be sober and are given a cigar and a whiskey and soda. They are both physically large men and they feel they have done just about everything that can be done in India and now regard the country as not big enough for them. "*Therefore* we are going away to be Kings," says Carnehan. They claim they have been thinking about it for months and have decided there is only one place to go.

They want to do a "Sar-a-wak". They have heard about the exploits of Sir James Brooke, known as 'the White Rajah', who had worked for the East India Company but who, in 1841, became Ruler of Sarawak and whose descendants ruled for some years after him. The two loafers, using that example, have chosen Kafiristan as their prospective kingdom."They have two-and-thirty heathen idols there and we'll be the thirty-third and fourth. It's a mountainous country, and the women of those parts are very beautiful." Carnehan reminds Dravot that the issue of women is covered in what they call 'the Contrack'. "Neither Woman nor Liqu-or, Daniel." [14] The "Contrack" is agreement between them to refrain from those pleasures if they are to become kings.

They are confident that their army training and ability to drill men will make them attractive to the local King. "Then we will subvert that King and seize his throne and establish a Dy-nasty". The narrator warns them that they have no chance of surviving such a journey and that no Englishman has been there. He provides them with his maps and an atlas so that they can examine the country and their route there. They are familiar with part of the road. "We was there with Roberts' Army." General Roberts (later Lord Roberts) had been a commander during the Second Afghan war of 1878-80 and had marched from Kabul to Kandahar. Kipling had written in his letters of his pride in riding into Simla side by side with General 'Bobs' Roberts.

As they pore over the maps and books about Kafiristan, Carnehan exclaims, "Dan, they're a stinkin' lot of heathens, but this book here says they think they're related to us English." This one line, as we will see, may go a long way to explain what happens later although it is easily missed as the story rushes forward. The two loafers boast, "When we've got our Kingdom in going order we'll let you know, and you can come and help us govern it."

The narrator dismisses them as fools and offers them money or help getting work. They claim that they only have one fear and that is "Drink" and they ask the narrator to witness the contract between the two whereby they determine to become Kings of Kafiristan and they swear to forgo drink and women and conduct themselves with "Dignity" and "Discretion" in the quest for their own little empire. The narrator leaves them in his office and departs, with an invitation from the two loafers to join them the following day at the Serai, the local meeting place where camels and horses are assembled and loaded for their journeys to all parts of Asia.

When the narrator arrives at the Serai the following day, the multitude are laughing at the antics of a mad priest. The penny drops and the narrator realizes that the priest in rags is Dravot, with Carnehan acting as his servant. Both men are disguised as natives. They ask the narrator to feel their camel-bags. They are full of Martini-

Henry rifles which were standard issue for the British military in India at this period. The guns are a valuable commodity, but also could attract unwelcome attention. Their intention is to join a regular caravan going through the Khyber Pass.[15]

As they begin to depart, Dravot asks the narrator, "Give us a memento of your kindness, *Brother*. You did me a service, yesterday, and that time in Marwar. Half my Kingdom shall you have, as the saying goes." The narrator slips a charm compass from his watch chain and hands it to the "priest". In the film version it is the sight of the charm on his watch chain that alerts Carnehan to the fact that the man whose pocket he has just picked is a Freemason. They say their farewells and the caravan departs. Ten days later the newspaper office hears a report that the mad priest has managed to go over the border into Afghanistan.

Two years pass in the newspaper office. It is another unbearably hot summer's night and again the narrator is working in the early hours of the morning. As he turns to leave "...present crept to my chair what was left of a man." The narrator continues, "I could hardly see whether he walked or crawled-this rag-wrapped, whining cripple who addressed me by name, crying that he was come back." The journalist does not recognize the man. "'I've come back,' he repeated; 'and I was King of Kafiristan- me and Dravot- crowned Kings we was!'" Recognition dawns on the narrator and the story unfolds.[16]

As their adventure begins, Carnehan describes how they reached Kafiristan and became Kings. They intervene in a fight between two groups of natives and demonstrate their ability with the rifle. Dravot pays his respect to the natives' idol and again they show their fighting skills to defeat an adjoining village in combat. Dravot, from the outset, behaves as if he is their king. Their military knowledge has helped establish their credibility. After only a short period, their kingdom has expanded so that Dravot is in command in one valley and Carnehan in another. Dravot appears in Carnehan's village wearing a gold crown and presents another for his partner. He is happy after weeks of fighting and marching and claims that every village within fifty miles is now peaceful.

Then suddenly the youthful Kipling runs riot again with Masonic ritual. "Peachey, says Dravot, we don't want to fight no more. The Craft's the trick, so help me!"[17] Dravot produces a native chief whom they have named Billy Fish, who, to his surprise knows Masonic ritual. (They give the natives names of people they knew from their days in India).

Dravot directs Carnehan to shake hands with Billy Fish. To Carnehans's amazement Billy Fish gives him the Fellowcraft's grip, the special handshake of the Second Degree. Carnehan asks whether he also knows the password that goes with the handshake and Dravot confirms that he does. "The Chiefs and the priests can work a Fellow Craft Lodge in a way that's very like ours, and they've cut the marks on the rocks, but they don't know the Third Degree, and they've come to find out."[18]

Amazingly Kipling asks his readers to accept this and offers no explanation as to how an obscure tribe in the North West came to know about Freemasonry, its different degrees, handshakes and passwords. Dravot and Carnehan feel very superior as they, like Kipling, have been through the third degree and these natives only know the first two degrees. Dravot has checked that Billy Fish does not know the third. Why this strange situation has arisen is not explained. Again it is not enough that they know about Freemasonry, but why this tribe should know two but not the three main craft ceremonies is a leap that Kipling asks his readers to make. There is a hint in some literature that Alexander the Great may have travelled through Kafiristan and perhaps Kipling is suggesting that the ritual may have been left behind at that time. That is also the explanation as to why the natives in the story are referred to as white or like the English, as there was a legend that as Alexander passed through this land he left issue whose descendants were still living there, and Kipling would most certainly have known about that legend.

When Carnehan confirms his discovery, Dravot enthuses: "It's the Gord's Truth. I've known these long years that the Afghans knew up to the Fellow Craft Degree but this is a miracle. A God and a Grandmaster of the Craft am I, and a Lodge in the Third Degree I will open, and we'll raise the head priests and the Chief of the Villages. " A moment of sanity is introduced by Carnehan. He warns Dravot, "It's against all the law," and continues, "holding a Lodge without a warrant from any one; and you know we never held office in any Lodge." Dravot is not interested in such a warning or caution. He feels everything is running for him."The temple of Imbra will do for a Lodge-room. The women must make aprons as you show them." Carnehan describes to the narrator the aprons that were made, with Dravot having a special one with turquoise lumps on hide. They also painted the black floor of the temple with white squares. On the night of the Lodge meeting Carnehan is worried that they would give away the fact that they didn't really know the ritual. At the very moment that Dravot puts on his apron the priests, affronted by the position that the adventurers are taking, are preparing to attack him.

But as the priests gather to overthrow the adventurers they are miraculously recued by another Masonic plot line. The priests, in their attack, overturn the heavy stone that Dravot has been using as the Grand Master's chair and on its underside the stone reveals a mark or symbol cut into it identical to the symbol that Dravot has displayed on his apron. The priests are shocked by this coincidence and the godlike status of the two men is confirmed.

Kipling knew all about marks and he would have received a certificate with his own mark on it from Grand Mark Lodge after he was advanced into that degree, but it seems he lost the certificate, as a duplicate of his Grand Mark Lodge certificate recording his specific mark was issued to him in May 1918.

Here Kipling has taken another bite of his Masonic education and introduced the Mark degree. He has gained his knowledge when he was advanced to be a Mark Mason while he was in Lahore. For those unfamiliar with it, the Mark degree is based around the story of the quarrying of stone for King Solomon's Temple. Each new advancee (new brother) to Mark Masonry is given a specific mark of his own to identify his work just as traditional masons did when building a cathedral. When that happened Kipling would have been given a specific mark usually based on his first or second initial. In Kipling's case, it was the shape of a "K". In the story that is enacted in the Mark ritual, every stone for the temple must be perfect and approved by the Overseers and once approved the stonemason's mark is engraved on it.

Dravot, using the butt of his gun as a gavel, declares, "By virtue of the authority vested in me by my own right hand and the help of Peachey, I declare myself Grand-Master of all Freemasonry in Kafiristan in this Mother Lodge o' the country, and King of Kafiristan equally with Peachey."[19] He appoints Carnehan as Senior Warden. He goes on to describe the Raising Ceremony. "It was not in any way according to the Ritual, but it served our turn. We didn't raise more than ten of the biggest men, because we didn't want to make the Degree common."

They then conduct a Third Degree ceremony from memory "not in any way according to the ritual."Freemasons reading this story may by now have developed considerable scepticism about Dravot and Carnehan's Masonic knowledge.

The two men enjoy a period of success during the next six months. Under their leadership their tribe conquers other adjoining villages. But these military victories go to Dravot's head and he starts to see himself as an Empire builder. He visualizes himself being knighted by Queen Victoria, and on a level with the Viceroy of India. Differences emerge between the two men, especially after Dravot determines to take a wife. Despite Carnehan reminding him of their pact to remain celibate and begging him not to take that risk, Dravot insists on finding a bride. The terrified woman chosen by him, thinking that marriage to a god will mean her instant death, bites him. He bleeds and his divine status is instantly destroyed.[20] The natives turn on them and despite help from Billy Fish, they pursue the two adventurers, with Dravot dying a brave but horrible death during the chase. Carnehan survives the chase but is crucified. Miraculously he does not die and his survival overnight impresses the natives sufficiently to release him, to return to Lahore to tell his tale.

Finally the crippled and bent Carnehan tells the narrator, "You knew Dravot, sir! You knew Right Worshipful Brother Dravot! Look at him now!" and he produces from his rags the shriveled head of Dravot still wearing his crown. At the end of the story Carnehan dies and no trace of the crown is found.

Some critics have interpreted this story as an analogy of the huge ambition of British imperialism during this period, and the crucifixion of Carnehan a reminder that British personnel were crucified during conflict in Burma in the 1880s. Cornell advances the theory that Dravot and Carnehan failed because everything they did was based upon deceit, especially their deceit of the natives over their Masonic role. [21] I think that in reality the young Kipling, enjoying his Freemasonry, used the experience of the meeting on the train and linked that to recent political and military events on the north eastern border of India to create an imaginative adventure story. The brilliance of its creation is shown by the fact that even after 125 years the story still generates the same excitement.

When John Huston, the film director, made the story into a successful film he cast Sean Connery and Michael Caine (who is apparently a Freemason) as the heroes Dravot and Carnehan. The two actors are well chosen for the parts as the two rough and ready former soldiers, and they possess the swagger that is needed to make the characters convincing. In the film, the narrator is portrayed as Kipling himself. The meeting on the train is retained but in this version Carnehan steals the narrator's watch which has a Masonic fob on the chain, and which, as a result he feels morally obliged to return. The early scenes in the film have the two soldiers calling Kipling "brother" and the cryptic exchange between Kipling and

Carnehan at the start of the story is kept intact, but one suspects the Masonic detail was a little too obscure for the screenwriter and much of it disappears.

The film was largely shot in Morocco and, whereas the natives in the original story were suggested by Kipling to be almost white, in the film they are distinctly dark. In the film the character of Billy Fish, the tribal leader, is translated into a Ghurka, and a translator and ally to Dravot and Carnehan. In the original story, Kipling left the reader wondering whether the story of their conquest was Carnehan's invention, but the film removes that dramatic uncertainty by leaving the grisly but still crowned head of Dravot in Kipling's office.

This story remains a popular topic of conversation among literary critics. Edmund Wilson saw it as a parable by Kipling about what would happen to the English if they lost their moral authority,[22] but this is may be too pompous an interpretation of an adventure story written by a twenty-three year-old. That might have been true of the later Kipling but when he wrote this story he was still full of the verve and the excitement of youth. Also, it fails to recognize that his interest in Freemasonry at that time fired his imagination.

Just as the adventures of Josiah Harlan may have been known to Kipling, there is another possible source for this adventure story.[23] Kipling, on one of his trips during his summer leave, had met Charlie Wilson whose father was known as Rajah Wilson or Wilson the Mountain Man. According to biographer Charles Allen, Wilson was believed to be a deserting British soldier who, after various adventures, went into the Himalayas and made a fortune out of timber, living for a while on his wits and the threat of his gun. Later two of Wilson's sons scandalized the native population by kidnapping two local women, which led to their being expelled from the mountains. It is quite likely that Kipling knew this story, either from meeting Charlie Wilson or having heard it second hand, and it combined perfectly with his experience on the train with the two Masonic loafers. It should be noted that in this story, and in *Kim*, the characters of Dravot and Carnehan and Kimball O'Hara, Kim's father, are hardly a credit to Freemasonry.

Kipling used Freemasonry to dramatic effect in several stories of this period. *The Rout of the White Hussars* in *Plain Tales from the Hills* has been mentioned earlier, but the craft also appeared in the collection known as *Soldiers Three*.[24] In the story *With the Main Guard* those three unforgettable soldiers, Otheris, Mulvaney and Learoyd recall a battle where the combatants were so tightly compressed together there was hardly room to swing a weapon. The hand to hand fighting is converted to an exchange of the words from the Third Degree ceremony.

Mulvaney describes their encounter with a group of Pathans. There wasn't room to use a rifle. He continues, "Nothin' but knife an' bay'nit when we cud get our hands free: and that was not often. We was breast-on to thim, an' the Tyrone was yelpin' behind av us in a way I didn't see the lean av at first. But I knew later, an' so did the Paythans.

'Knee to knee!' sings out Crook, (their Captain) wid a laugh whin the rush av our comin' into the gut shtopped, an' he was huggin' a hairy great Paythan, neither bein' able to do anything to the other, tho' both was wishful.

'Breast to breast!' he sez, as the Tyrone was pushin' us forward closer an' closer.

'An' hand over back!' sez a Sargint that was behin'. I saw a sword lick out past Crook's ear like a snake's tongue, an' the Paythan was tuk in the apple av his throat like a pig at Dromeen fair.

'Thank ye, Brother Inner Guard,' sez Crook, cool as a cucumber widout salt."

I wonder whether there are any other examples of Masonic ritual being called out during the heat of hand to hand combat. I doubt it!

CHAPTER FIVE

KIM

While Kipling was a master of the short story, he often seemed to struggle with the larger canvas provided by a full scale novel. Some of his novels - *Captain Courageous* and *The Light that Failed* - have identifiable weaknesses, but few can challenge the success of *Kim*. It is a book that can appeal to any age group. Some readers have revisited it time and time again. It can be read as a pure adventure story or seen at a more profound level as a spiritual quest. His critics, voluble as always, are by no means unanimous but in this case the detractors are in a distinct minority. Indian writer Nirad Chaudhari called it the finest story about India in English.[1] The depth of detail is vast. There is certainly nothing else in English literature to compare with it. Kipling is the only major figure in English letters who had had the knowledge and experience of India, which gives the novel its authentic period atmosphere. His years as a journalist had given him contact with every strata of Indian and Anglo-Indian society. Perhaps the only other English writer to capture the essence of India was E.M.Forster, who did so a generation later, but the Oxford-educated Forster could not be more different to Kipling. He lacked the advantage of Indian birth and those early formative and teenage years. He also wrote at a time when the break between Britain and India and the drive for Indian independence was becoming stronger. Most of Forster's experience was with the upper echelons of Indian society.

Though it may have been based on an earlier, lost tale called 'Mother Maturin', *Kim* was conceived in Vermont in 1892, some four years after Kipling left India, and it was finished much later while he was living in Sussex. The first version was illustrated by Lockwood, who contributed to the concept and the vivid ingredients of the story. Kipling recalls in his autobiography, how his father helped him verify the detail, which adds so much to the success of the book. Kipling's regard for his father is unquestionable, and in his autobiography he calls him an "expert fellow-craftsman." [2] The novel appeared in 1901, twelve years after Kipling had left India, but it conveys an enduring panorama of fin de siècle India, portraying the country from the viewpoint of the Raj, but without neglecting life from the native standpoint. It is also rooted in Kipling's childhood, and his teenage and early twenties experiences. It describes British Imperial India at its zenith, before the decline of the Raj became irreversible. The Mutiny of 1857 was still uncomfortably close, but the militant cry for independence had only just acquired its voice with the establishment of the Congress Party in 1880. It also describes much of India physically- its geography, peoples, customs and politics. It demonstrates the religious differences, the tensions with Russia on the northern borders, and the colour and vitality of a country already teeming with a massive population.

Kipling as a child, and later as a teenage journalist, had absorbed India. It was in his blood and, although he only returned briefly to India once, it stayed in his work for the rest of his life. Angus Wilson described *Kim* as "a love letter to India."[3] Kipling is sometimes reviled for being the spokesman and apologist for the Empire, but a more balanced explanation is put forward by the eminent Orientalist scholar Edward Said. Commenting specifically on *Kim*, he said, ".....whether we like the fact or not, we should regard its author as writing not just from the dominating viewpoint of a white man describing a colonial possession, but also from the perspective of a massive colonial system whose economy, functioning and history had acquired the status almost of a fact of nature."[4] At the point that Kipling worked as a journalist in India, the British presence had lasted over two hundred years and still had half of a century to run, and was in many ways totally embedded in Indian life.

A Kipling admirer who spent some time working in India was Malcolm Muggeridge, who felt that Kipling "represents the only truly artistic yield of the years of the British Raj..." Muggeridge considered that the Indians were more appreciative of Kipling than his fellow countrymen, "whose judgement was twisted and distorted by excessive guilt feelings about ever having ruled over India at all, and who, in the present climate of opinion , (Muggeridge was writing in the early 1970s) would rather appear as rapists than as racialists."[5] Even allowing for Muggeridge's left-wing sympathies there is an element of truth in this.

If you are an admirer of *Kim,* you see the whole story as a demonstration by Kipling of his enduring love of India. He catches the colour and sound and light of India. Kim, the main character, is a lovable waif- "the Little Friend of all the World". The story is peopled by traders, peasants, horse dealers, soldiers, spies, and shopkeepers, as he and the Teshoo Lama travel the Great Trunk Road, spanning the country, with the Lama seeking the mystical river of purification, which will be the culmination of his religious quest. One wonders whether the idea for seeking that lost river might have been derived from the concept of the lost Masonic secrets with which Kipling would have been familiar.

Kipling was not the son of a soldier, but he was steeped in the life and culture of the Raj. He had mixed at the highest levels of the government and administration, but he also knew the natives, the ordinary soldiers and sometimes the seedier side of Indian life. He saw the inherent conflicts between the English masters and their subservient natives. Kipling himself said the book was plotless. He was perhaps being a little unkind to his own efforts, for there is a distinct story-line, but it is secondary to the development of the characters.

It is also a story of identity, and the conflict felt by Kim as he tried to reconcile his own identity as a the son of a sahib against the deep love he has developed for the Lama, and for the Indians to whom he feels so close. The book also contrasts Kim's search for his own identity with the Lama's search for his spiritual Nirvana. It might also reflect Kipling's own confusion with his identity. He was born in India and spent many of his formative years there. It is clear from his own writings that he never felt he was a complete Englishman. To Kipling, England was always something of a foreign country. But for the bitter quarrel with his brother-in-law he might have remained in America permanently.

Professor Karim described it: "The whole book is like a precious tapestry where the diversity of cultures, races and religions has magnificently synthesized to project the Masonic vision."[6] By the 1880s, India had partially recovered from but not forgotten the deep hatreds created by the Mutiny in 1857. Before Kipling departed India to enjoy his fame in England, the political opposition to British Imperial domination had started to become more vociferous. Are Kipling's descriptions of people and Indian life racist and condescending or is it an affectionate portrayal? The debate on this issue has divided critics and will probably never end. As a child and young man Kipling knew Lahore well, and that is reflected in Kim's acquaintance with its alleys and back streets. Kim is an orphan waif and almost classless. At the start of the novel, the boy straddles the Muslim and Hindu communities. He may have the background of a sahib (of which, at the start of the novel he is unaware) but he mixes easily with both Hindus and Muslims. He has no understanding of what it may mean to be a sahib. He is optimistic but wary. From Kipling's early childhood experiences it would seem that he was more comfortable with different levels of Indian society than many of his English contemporaries.

Theories have been advanced on the model for the boy Kim - the offspring of the marriage of a British soldier and white nursemaid. While Kipling was briefly a member of the Punjab Volunteers, he would have been commanded by a Colonel Goulding who, according to the expert on Kipling's India, Charles Allen, saw, at this period, a boy of a similar background. "Hatless and barefooted, with the cunning of a street Arab, this boy roamed about at will, and anything he did not know about the bazaar was not worth knowing…".[7] With the great numbers of British soldiers who were based in India, it is hardly surprising that there were children who were left either after the death of their parent, or simply abandoned. As we have seen earlier Kipling would also have known about these orphan children through his involvement as Charity Steward of his Lodge.

We first meet Kim in the novel sitting astride the giant gun Zam –Zammah in Lahore, (it stands there to this day.) outside the museum where, in real life, Lockwood Kipling had been the curator. Kim is a "poor white boy" - a child grown up in the back streets and bazaars of Lahore after the death of his parents. His mother had died giving birth to him. "Burned black as any native", he is nonetheless the son of an Irish colour sergeant, Kimball O'Hara, who stayed in India, when his regiment returned to Ireland. After leaving the army O'Hara had worked on the railways, but, like many Europeans in nineteenth century India, he succumbed to opium, leaving Kim as an orphan, to be cared for by a kindly half-caste woman. As we see Kim's lifestyle in the first part of the novel, he is completely at home with the natives, who treat him as one of their own. He moves easily between Hindu and Muslim communities, but from the very first few lines, Kipling leaves us in no doubt that Kim is European. It is interesting that in both *Kim* and *The Man Who Would Be King* Kipling chose characters who had become "losers" after their military service was completed but are partially redeemed (and only partially) by the fact they were Freemasons.

Kim's sole possessions, and the key to the whole narrative, are his father's Masonic "ne varietur", his clearance certificate and his birth certificate; documents he doesn't understand but knows are valuable. His father had told him that they "belonged to a great piece of magic- as men practiced over yonder behind the Museum in the big blue-and-white Jadoo-Gher- the magic house, as we name the Masonic Lodge."[8] His father had told him that "it would all come right some day and Kim's horn would be exalted between pillars-monstrous pillars- of strength and beauty." His father had told Kim as small child that one day the Colonel of the regiment would attend to Kim, together with nine hundred first class devils, whose God was a Red Bull on a green field.

His father promised Kim that he would be better off than him, but the story and explanation meant little or nothing to the small child. After his father's death, the half-caste woman had sewn the documents into a leather amulet case, which Kim kept strung around his neck. However the woman also knew that if she sent Kim to the Jadoo-Gher, he would be taken over by the Provincial Grand Lodge and sent to the Masonic school. She distrusted magic, and refused to do that. Kim himself is cautious and suspicious of missionaries and white men.

He is known in the bazaars of Lahore as "Little Friend of all the World" and knows every inch of the back street alleys as he runs errands, and relishes the intrigue. This is all part of an education that will hold him in good stead as the narrative develops.

At the start of the story, Kim meets the Holy Man – an elderly Tibetan Lama who is searching for the Holy River which "washes away all sins". Buddhists believe that the Buddha had shot an arrow, and where that arrow landed a river formed and became holy. Kim agrees to accompany him as his "chela" – his disciple, and to beg for food for them.[9] The central part of the narrative describes Kim's journeys and adventures with the holy Lama. While doing that, Kim also carries messages for his friend, a Muslim horse dealer, Mahbub Ali, who, we later learn, is a spy for the British. This is Kim's introduction to deeper intrigue and the Great Game. It is a journey of discovery for both Kim and the Lama. Here Kipling takes the story on two levels. He combines the story of the lama's spiritual search for his holy River of the Arrow with his disciple's search for his identity, which ultimately depends on his father's Masonic papers.

The theme of seeking for lost secrets by the Lama, and the mythical River of the Arrow, does have echoes of Freemasons seeking for the lost secrets of Hiram Abiff. The search by both the Lama and Kim are also journeys of self-realization. Again there is a Masonic resonance with the exhortation to seek "knowledge of yourself" urged upon Masonic candidates.[10] Like so much of Kipling's work, there is always the contrast – in this case between the godly and the secular. The Lama's search is spiritual, and Kim's a very practical one. It is also the story of the growing relationship between an elderly man and a boy. The Lama exerts his spiritual influence, and in some ways becomes the father that Kim never really had.

At the start of his journey with the Lama, Kim is thirteen. Early in his travels with the Lama, he sees a banner displayed at a military encampment bearing a Red Bull on a Green background, and in crawling closer to see it, he is discovered by members of his father's old regiment, the Mavericks.[11] He is caught by the regiment's two padres, his *ne varietur,* clearance certificate and baptismal certificate are discovered, and his paternity established. His father may only have been a humble soldier, but he had been a Freemason, and the two priests knew him well. In addition, Kim's father had scrawled on the certificate many times, "Look after the boy. Please look after the boy", adding his name and regimental number.

His captors, who are the regiment's Anglican and Roman Catholic chaplains, discuss what they must do with Kim. Kipling treats the two priests very differently. "We cannot allow an English boy - assuming he is the son of Mason, the sooner he goes to the Masonic Orphanage the better", says Mr. Bennett, the Anglican priest who is also secretary of the Regimental Lodge.[12] Bennett is painted by Kipling in a very harsh light, while Father Victor, the Roman Catholic priest, warms to both Kim and the Lama. Both Father Victor and Bennett, although enjoying a degree of mutual respect, also understand each other's motives and each wants to promote their own brand of Christianity. If Kim goes to the Masonic Orphanage, he will be brought up as a Protestant. The Lama, now involved in discussion with the two priests, is distressed at the prospect of losing his disciple, but at this point he discovers that Kim is a Sahib and that he now has the opportunity of a proper education. The regimental priests make it clear that they will not allow Kim to accompany the Lama any further on his journey. (One wonders where that authority was derived.)

The Roman Catholic Father Victor is not only a more sympathetic character than Reverend Arthur Bennett, his Anglican counterpart, but he also recognizes the Lama's spirituality and sincerity. Bennett is disdainful of the Buddhist holy man. He looks at him "with the triple-ringed uninterest of the creed that lumps nine-tenths of the world under the title 'heathen.' " The Lama may be one of the most sensitive figures that Kipling created. There is always an air of saintliness and mystery about him, yet after only a few days together the aged monk and his young, increasingly worldly wise companion, have already developed a deep bond of affection.

Father Victor tells the Lama that the best education to be had in India is at St Xavier's in Lucknow - not surprisingly a Catholic school, rather than the Punjab Masonic Orphanage. The Lama asks the amount of the fees there, and undertakes to pay them. Although Father Victor is sceptical of his ability to pay, he accepts the Lama's offer. Kim's immediate fate is settled, and the Lama departs to continue his spiritual quest, leaving Kim in the custody of his father's regiment. What Kipling makes clear is that Kim has received very favourable treatment, and that would not have been the case if his father had not been a member of the Lodge and in good standing. As was described in Chapter Two, Lodges were providing for orphaned children, and Kipling had been Charity Steward of his Lodge. He would also have known that regimental Lodges took on similar responsibilities.[13]

During this period Britain kept tens of thousands of soldiers in India and most regiments had their own travelling military Lodge. Although there is no direct evidence that Kipling visited these Lodges, several met at the military encampment at Mian Mir near Lahore, where Kipling certainly went as part of his journalist duties. The Lodge of St. John the Evangelist No.1483 met there. That Lodge had, amongst its members, a Captain Terence Mulvaney and a Lieutenant Learoyd - later to become the surnames of two of the characters in Kipling's *Soldiers Three* stories, which had been written while he was still working in India. It is almost certain that Kipling visited this Lodge.

While Kim is waiting to be sent off to school in Lucknow, he manages to get a letter to his friend Mahbub Ali, hoping he may rescue him from his enforced education. Within a day or so, the horse dealer arrives, closely followed by a Colonel Creighton, who purports to be head of the Ethnological Survey for India. Mahbub Ali extols Kim's abilities to the Colonel, who also makes enquiries of Father Victor. He reports that he has already received from the Lama a note drawn on an Indian bank, in payment of the school fees. Father Victor is rather overwhelmed by everything that has happened concerning Kim."It's this mixture of Red Bulls and Rivers of Healing (poor heathen, God help him!) an' notes of hand and Masonic certificates. Are you a Mason, by any chance?", he asks Creighton.[14]

"By Jove, I am, now I come to think of it. That's an additional reason," responds Creighton, apparently remembering his Masonic obligation to help the offspring of a deceased brother. The Colonel also says that the Regiment will pay for Kim's school outfit, thus saving the Lodge that expense. Significantly, Creighton also offers to accompany Kim to his new school in Lucknow.

The three day journey to the school is Creighton's opportunity to start the serious education of his pupil, ostensibly to be a surveyor for the government, but, in reality, to test Kim's potential as a spy and to teach him the basics of his future craft. He also admonishes Kim that, although he is a Sahib, he must never deride the Indian. Creighton is clearly contemptuous of those Englishmen who despise the natives. This is an unqualified response to those who have claimed that Kipling was a racist. The journey with Creighton is also the first time that Kim starts to analyse his own identity. Is he a Sahib or is he a native? "Who is Kim?" he asks himself. That debate will continue.

Having met the Lama again, who is waiting for him when he arrives at his school, Kim gradually becomes reconciled to the advantages of education, provided that in the vacations he can escape and briefly resume his native identity. Over the next three years, Kim spends his vacation time with Lurgan Sahib, who becomes his tutor for the Great Game, operating from his shop in Simla, and with horse-trader Mahbub Ali on the road. By now, it is quite clear that Kim is being trained to become one of Creighton's men on the "survey of India", and that his activities will provide an excellent cover for his work as a spy. He also meets another of Creighton's spies, Huree Babu. At sixteen Kim is released from school, provided with his basic spying kit, and told he can be free for six months to go and rejoin the Lama on his travels. Kim's adventures start almost immediately, and his newly taught skills are put to the test.

Mahbub Ali takes him to see a strange blind woman, Huneefa, who has a special dye that will colour Kim's skin, so that he can pass for a lengthy period as a native. She also casts spells over Kim. Huree Babu then gives him the clothes that he will wear as he resumes his role as the Lama's disciple. During Kim's time at school, the Lama has continued his wanderings in search of the mystic river.

As part of his training as a spy, Huree has the task of briefing Kim on what he should do if he finds himself in a tough corner. He says to Kim, "You say 'I am Son of the Charm'. He continues, "As I was about to say, 'Son of the Charm' means that you may be a member of the *Sat Bhai*- the Seven Brothers, which is Hindi *and* Tantric. It is popularly supposed to be an extinct Society, but I have written notes to show it is still extant. You see, it is all my invention. Verree good. Sat Bhai has many members, and perhaps before they jolly-well-cut-your-throat they may give you a chance of life." He then gives Kim a test sentence that Kim has to repeat. He must be very precise in saying this sentence. He warns him, "You are on acting-allowance [i.e. Kim has only been appointed on a probationary basis] you see: so if you are called upon to help Sons of the Charm mind you jolly well try."[15] Within a few days, Kim has to put that teaching into practice in a life and death situation to help a fellow agent in danger.

It seems that the Sons of the Charm, are pure Kipling invention, but again with distinctive Masonic overtones. [16] There can be little doubt that the idea for the Sons was born from Kipling's Masonic experiences. As Kim's travels and adventures with the Lama continue, he does have use for Huree's Sons of the Charms. In the latter part of the book, the mature Kim, while accompanying the now declining and elderly Lama, finds his training for the Great Game put to vital use. Kipling constantly combines the excitement generated by the espionage storyline with the deepening of the relationship between the two characters. Kim is increasingly devoted to his spiritual guide, and the Lama's love for Kim deepens, despite the fact that he is now acknowledged as a white man and a Sahib. The closing pages of dialogue between the white boy and the Tibetan monk merit close attention, as the boy abases himself before the monk.

I have covered only a fraction of the events and characters in this book and concentrated on its Masonic links, but I suggest that Freemasons who read it will derive even more from it than the average reader, especially knowing the origins of the story. His biographers have shown that Kipling wanted for many years to write a novel about India, and started and put aside an earlier version of what became *Kim*. Years later, he was able to put his breadth of experience in India into this setting, and distill it with his Masonic career to produce this masterpiece. Although some may disagree, *Kim* is entitled to be treated as one of the great English classics. It displays great imagination, adventure, sense of period, captivating characters. It brings India to life, and particularly the contrast between the spiritual and the secular worlds that India constantly creates

Kim has reached the cinema twice. Hollywood tackled it in 1952, with Dean Stockwell playing Kim, Errol Flynn as a dashing and charming red-bearded but rather European Mahbub Ali and Paul Lukas as the Lama. In this version, the main story line is preserved although, like many screen treatments, sub-plots and characters have to be radically reduced. Kim still gets his identity from the papers in the amulet he wears around his neck, except that the Masonic references in the documents have been removed from the film's script in their entirety. Nineteen fifties Technicolour brings the Grand Trunk Road vividly to life.

A generation later, in 1984, a doddery Peter O'Toole, wearing a ghastly wig, which made him resemble Jimmy Savile, played the Lama, with Australian Brian Brown as an amorous Mahbub Ali and Ravi Sheth as Kim. Sheth is almost too Indian for Kim (the film makers seemed to have forgotten that the whole point of the story is that Kim is a white boy), and again a swashbuckling Mahbub is effective, but not in the least Indian. The main narrative elements of the original are retained but there are new sub-plots introduced, including a deserting soldier who has an affair with an Indian woman - not an element of which Kipling would necessarily have approved. This film sank without trace. In this version the Masonic connection was also completely removed. The writers of the script for both films failed to appreciate that the Regiment's interest in Kim, and their desire to see him properly educated came mainly from the fact that his late father had been a member of the regimental Lodge. Without that Masonic connection the story would have developed very differently. Perhaps the final verdict on both film versions is that it would be very difficult for any film to do justice to the depth, detail and subtleties of the book; and that a great book deserved a better screen treatment.

As an indication of Kipling's prodigious memory, it should be remembered that Kim was written more than a decade after he left India, yet that is a minor feat in comparison to his recollection of childhood reading which he was still able to recall more than twenty-five years later. Following this theme, it may have been a Masonic link and recollection that inspired *The Jungle Books*. Writing to the publisher Edward Routledge in 1897, Kipling asks him if he can recall who wrote a story that appeared in a boy's annual circa 1872-75.[17] Kipling continues, "It concerned a man who wandered into the interior of Africa and there met a lion who (to the man's no small amazement) gave him a Masonic sign. On the strength of this little variation from the normal, he struck up a friendship with the lion, his family and the rest of the lion-people and discovered that their deadly enemies were some dog-headed (and entirely unMasonic) baboons with whom he and the lions fought a furious fight". Kipling asks Routledge to identify the story for him. Pinney in his footnotes to the Kipling letters identifies it as a story called *King Lion* by James Greenwood, which appeared in *Boys' Own Magazine* in 1864. Kipling later confirmed he had read this during his miserable time in Southsea.

Kipling refers to the same story in his autobiography.[18] He describes how, during his first American winter in Bliss Cottage, the heavy snow gave him ample time to write. He wrote a story about a boy who had been brought up by wolves. "In the stillness, and suspense, of the winter of '92 some memory of the Masonic Lions of my childhood magazine, and a phrase in Haggard's *Nada the Lily*, combined with the echo of this tale." Thus Mowgli and the Jungle Books were born.

The Banner of Rudyard Kipling Lodge No.8169 which meets at Battle in Sussex.

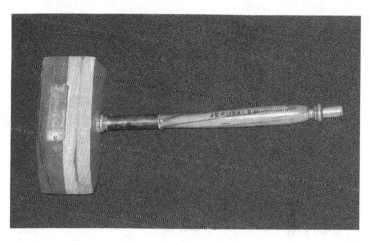

The Kipling Gavel from Grand River Lodge No.151, Kitchener, Ontario.

The Petition for Lodge Builders of the Silent Cities No.4948 including the signature of Rudyard Kipling.

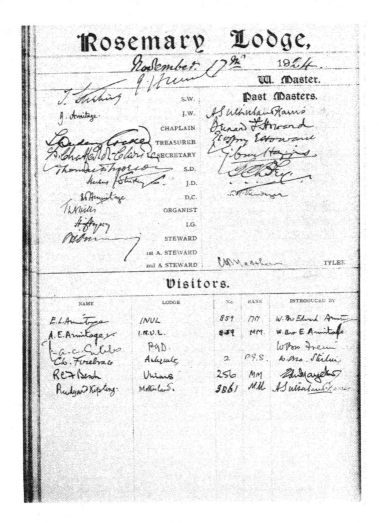

Kipling's signature shown in the Tyler's Book of Rosemary Lodge No.2851, his only recorded visit to an English Lodge.

LODGE " KHYBER," No. 582, PESHAWAR,
(WOR. BRO. J. W. DAVIES, STEWARD.)

				Rs. A. P.	Rs. A. P.
SUMS UNDER Rs. 12—credited to Lodge :—					
J. Cooper, Esquire	...	...	...	3 0 0	
E. B. Ettbridge, Esquire	...	...	...	3 0 0	
R. E. Sakloth, ,,	...	...	...	3 0 0	
E. Dosabhoy, ,,	...	...	...	1 0 0	
M. Litchfield, ,,	...	...	...	5 0 0	
J. Wachsel, ,,	...	...	...	2 0 0	
G. Cocks, ,,	...	...	...	2 0 0	
H. Bailey, ,,	...	...	...	2 0 0	
T. C. Craig, ,,	...	...	...	2 0 0	
J. W. Davies, ,,	...	...	...	5 0 0	
Messrs. Jehangir & Co.	...	...	...	10 0 0	
					38 0 0
Lieut. W. D. Stuart	...	...	...	...	30 0 0
H. Rogers, Esquire	...	...	...	...	12 0 0
			TOTAL Rs.	...	80 0 0

LODGE " HOPE AND PERSEVERANCE, No. 782, LAHORE,
(BRO. J. RUDYARD KIPLING, STEWARD.)

				Rs. A. P.	Rs. A. P.
Lodge " Hope and Perseverance" No. 782			...	...	50 0 0
SUMS UNDER Rs. 12—credited to Lodge :—			...		
The Revd. W. Briggs	...	...	...	5 0 0	
					5 0 0
A. B. Phelan, Esquire, B. A., C. E.	...	...	...	...	12 0 0
Colonel O. Menzies	...	...	...	...	16 0 0
Revd. F. J. Montgomery, M. A.	...	...	...	...	12 0 0
J. J. Davies, Esquire	...	...	...	...	12 0 0
F. Koenig, ,,	...	...	...	...	16 0 0
E. Sparling, ,,	...	...	...	...	12 0 0
H. Rotton, ,,	...	...	...	...	12 0 0
E. A. Gillon, ,,	...	...	...	...	12 0 0
W. Bull, ,,	...	...	...	...	30 0 0
General G. B. Wolseley, C. B. S.B.C.	...	...	...	...	50 0 0
E. Gruhn, Esquire	...	...	...	...	12 0 0
D. A Spankie, Esquire	...	...	...	...	12 0 0
H. W. Varmington, Esquire	...	...	...	...	12 0 0
C. Brown, Esquire	...	...	...	...	24 0 0
			TOTAL Rs.	...	299 0 0

The Charity Account for Lodge Hope & Perseverance
No.782(E.C.) when Kipling was Charity Steward.

A Past Master's Jewel from Lodge Independence with Philanthropy, No.391(E.C.) Allahabad of which Kipling was a member.

A Past Master's Jewel of Kipling's Mother Lodge , Hope
& Perseverance No.782 (E.C.),Lahore.

The Annual Return of Lodge Hope & Perseverance No. 782 for 1896 signed by Rudyard Kipling as Secretary.

Kipling's global influence- a plaque in Sydney Harbour
photographed by the author in October 2010.

CHAPTER SIX
DEBITS AND CREDITS

Kipling published volumes of short stories throughout his career, but *Debits and Credits* (1926) deserves special attention for the major influence Freemasonry plays in four of these narratives. It was his penultimate collection. If one reviews the whole range of Kipling's short stories, he can perhaps be claimed as one of the greatest writers of short fiction in the English language. Although he wrote several novels, only *Kim* has acquired an enduring reputation, but in the more abbreviated form he found a medium where he has not been surpassed. He learnt this art on the *Civil and Military Gazette,* where he had a strict limit on available space for his tales and he developed the ability to narrate the story with brevity, but with no loss of dramatic tension or literary quality. In a Kipling story, every word counts. He established his reputation by the stories he wrote in India as a youngster. He added to those with the wonderful range of stories in the *Jungle Books,* but he continued to develop his art into his sixties. Every collection contains memorable stories.

One of the questions that biographers and critics have not satisfactorily answered is why, in this late collection of stories, he turned so frequently to Freemasonry as a vital element in the story. Freemasonry had featured in his early stories in India, when he was involved in the Craft in his twenties but, apart from relatively minor references, and use of Masonic terminology, (see Chapter 8), he had had no active involvement in the Craft for over 30 years. Yet without some appreciation of Freemasonry much of the subtlety of these later stories might be lost. Kipling was not a man who wrote carelessly, or without deep thought. Every line was carefully crafted, and so much was based on his own experiences and meticulous research. When we read the stories described in this chapter, we must believe that Kipling wrote because he had decided that Freemasonry had something to contribute - not only in overcoming the traumas and horrors of the First World War, but in his own search for some logic and balance, in what often appeared a hostile world.

The later stories are frequently neglected as they are more demanding on the reader. They are not the simple tales of life under the Raj. One can hardly compare the young bachelor of the 1880s with the serious middle-aged man in his fifties and sixties, damaged by two wars and the two family tragedies that had befallen him. However, the later stories repay the time invested in them. Kipling had always refined and edited his stories, but he became even more economical and succinct. Often he would keep a draft by him for years, constantly editing, refining and distilling it. No phrase is surplus and this often adds to the intensity. There is no fat on a Kipling story, in fact occasionally he could overdo this terseness and leave his reader puzzled and struggling with a cryptic reference.

Like all his work, the stories are shot through with his exceptional flair for the English language and the variety and subject range is unmatched. It is hardly surprising that he is our most quoted writer after Shakespeare. He had an uncanny knack of finding a phrase or sentiment that was utterly fresh and memorable. He could also capture a mood and encapsulate that in a phrase.

After the First World War Kipling appears, to some observers, an almost broken man. The loss of John and the uncertainty about his fate, weighed heavily on him and on Caroline. *Debits and Credits*, which includes some stark and harsh stories about suffering and bereavement, may have provided a catharsis for Kipling. It contains flashes of Kipling's humour and irreverence. It also allowed the author, like his characters, a route to escape from the suffering of war. It is within these stories that Kipling returns to Freemasonry for comfort. Obviously many of Kipling's stories have a basis in some experience he had undergone. What inspired him to write a series of stories built around servicemen in London attending an unofficial Lodge during the First World War? None of his biographers have offered any answer to that question.

One clue can be found in his correspondence. Professor Pinney notes the recollection of Lord Crawford and Balcarres, who met Kipling at a dinner at the Café Royal. Pinney quotes his Lordship as saying, in his own memoirs, that Kipling told him that he used to listen to soldiers in railway stations and would then write down their stories. [1] Kipling added that he was not sure what he should do with some of the stories that he heard. We also know of the enormous research that Kipling did in the six years he researched and wrote his two volume history of the Irish Guards. He had accumulated a mass of information about the War, and he used some of these ideas in the later stories.[2] In fact, the stories described in this chapter all start or are set within an informal or unwarranted Lodge in London, during or shortly after the First World War.

Although there had been Masonic references in many of his works, in this period they are much more concentrated, and Freemasonry becomes the subject, rather than a convenient form of expression. Angus Wilson, in an excellent biography of Kipling, wrote, "It is most interesting that, when he wanted, in his last years, to bring a variety of men together, to emphasize the underlying fellowship of humanity, to give men some bond of play and ritual that could relieve them from the necessary but confining disciplines of caste and rank and class and race which keep anarchy at bay, he should have turned to the Freemasonry which had been one of his principal releases from the sharp divisions of British India."[3] Wilson is the only biographer who makes the valuable point that, when Kipling was transferred by his employer from Lahore to Allahabad, he chose to enter the only Lodge that had many non-Europeans as its members. Wilson, however, does not restrain himself from criticizing these "Masonic" stories - "Kipling's extraordinary economic craftsmanship is lost in prolixity."[4]

Of the fourteen stories in this volume, first published together in 1926, four have their framework provided by a Masonic Lodge. Kipling used different devices as a setting for his tales and often the initial scene was to provide a framework or forum for a narrator to tell a tale within a tale. In these stories we witness the brethren gather for a ceremony or banquet, or even to clean the Lodge furniture, and one brother reminisces or relates one of his war time experiences. That leads on to the real narrative. Several of the brethren appear in more than one story, especially Bro. Burges who is clearly the driving force behind the fictional Lodge. Whether Burges or the Narrator is Kipling's voice is not always clear, but there is an element of Kipling in both of them. Burges, like Kipling, has lost a son in the War, and it seems that Masonry is the only interest and comfort he has left.

In his last two collections of stories Kipling wrote eight stories which in some way describe the effects that the War had had on servicemen. It is only in the first of those stories, *In the Interests of the Brethren,* that the whole story, is about the Lodge itself and little else. The stories themselves have little in common other than that they originate from talk between Brethren at a Lodge meeting, but they all point to Masonry as a comfort and solace to soldiers damaged physically and mentally by the War, and to the restorative benefits of ritual. *The Janeites* is a witty story, where a tongue in cheek Kipling uses the novels and characters of Jane Austen as the basis for a Lodge and ritual. *A Madonna of the Trenches* is a supernatural tale, deriving from warfare in the trenches, and finally in *A Friend of the Family,* the Lodge is the background to a story of friendship and revenge arising from the War. The four stories are very distinct, but the link is Freemasonry.

There is one other Masonic story entitled *Fairy Kist*, contained in his final collection, Limits *and Renewals.*

In the Interests of the Brethren

Set during the First World War, this story was written in 1917. Like most of Kipling's stories, it was published in a magazine and later brought together as part of a collection. It is prefaced by a poem, called *Banquet Night,* which is almost completely Masonic in derivation. It is a jolly poem stressing the egalitarian nature of Masonry and linking it to one of Kipling's other great loves - the naval officers' mess.

The poem starts:

'Once in so often,' King Solomon said,
Watching his quarrymen drill the stone,
'We will club our garlic and wine and bread,
And banquet together beneath my throne.
And all the Brethren shall come to that mess
As Fellow-Craftsmen- no more and no less.

As if to leave no doubt as to his Mark Masonry credentials, the last two stanzas conclude:

So it was ordered and so it was done,
And the hewers of wood and the Masons of Mark,
With foc'sle hands of the Sidon run,
And Navy Lords from the Royal Ark,
Came and sat down and were merry at mess,
As Fellow-Craftsmen- no more and no less.

The Quarries are hotter than Hiram's forge,
No one is safe from the dog-whips' reach.
It's mostly snowing up Lebanon gorge,
And it's always blowing off Joppa beach;
But once in so often, the messenger brings
Solomon's mandate: 'Forget these things!
Brother to Beggars and Fellow to Kings,
Companion of Princes-forget these things!
Fellow-Craftsman, forget these things!'

Lines similar to those in the last stanza, "Brother to a Prince and fellow to a beggar if he be found worthy," appear immediately after the title of the story *The Man Who Would be King*. *In the Interests of the Brethren* was written shortly after Kipling had joined the War Graves Commission (as it was then called), and six months after he had agreed to write the history of John's regiment, the Irish Guards. The story was first published in *Story -Teller and Metropolitan* in December 1918. The magazine commented about the story, "The motif which lies behind it is such that we urge all those who have relatives in the War who are Freemasons to send them a copy."

During the First World War Freemasonry, like many other activities, was seriously disrupted. Grand Lodge instructed Lodges not to penalize brethren on active service over unpaid subscriptions. Resolutions of Grand Lodge also urged strict economy on brethren in the consumption of food. [5] Interestingly the then Senior Grand Warden was also Minister of Food! Grand Lodge also recommended that brethren of German, Austrian, Hungarian and Turkish origins should not attend meetings for the duration of the war- a move that was not universally popular. Many Masons became prisoners of war, and as early as December 1914 the Grand Secretary received handwritten greetings and a request for relief and assistance from over 150 brethren who were held as prisoners of war in a concentration camp at Ruhleben, Spandau. Funds were immediately utilized to send parcels to those brethren.[6] During the First World War there was not the repression of Freemasonry that came later, under the Nazis.

After the War, Grand Lodge regularized some of the informal Lodges that had been convened during the conflict. There were informal Lodges at some of the prisoner of war camps. In particular two Lodges were actually consecrated in prison camps in Holland during the War. [7] Gastvrijheid No.3970 and Willem van Orange No.3976 were warranted originally, with the permission of the Germans, by the Grand East of the Netherlands, whose brethren were allowed to enter the camp. After the War both Lodges were granted English warrants and exist up to the present day. Two Lodges were established by servicemen during the war: Maguncor Lodge No. 3806 (Machine Gun Corps) and United Arts Rifles No. 3817, both formed in 1917.

Much of the content of the Quarterly Communications of Grand Lodge during the First World War relates to the War. In 1915, in enforcing the resolution that anyone of German origin should not attend, Grand Lodge expressed its horror at the crimes of which the Germans were guilty. Grand Lodge in 1917 debated a resolution relating to military Lodges, which it felt had become almost obsolete.[8] These were not Lodges like those mentioned above, but mobile Lodges travelling with military units in the field (like the regimental Lodge referred to earlier in *Kim*.) Such Lodges had existed since the early eighteenth century. As part of that discussion, they removed the embargo that had previously existed on men below the rank of corporal being initiated. Grand Lodge felt it was not only discriminatory but also wrong, as these potential candidates were putting their lives at risk for their country. Whether Kipling knew this rule is speculation, but fortunately Kim's father was a colour sergeant, and therefore eligible to join the regimental Lodge.

There is no evidence that any Lodge or Lodge of Instruction similar to Kipling's Faith and Works No. 5837 actually existed in London during the First World War. Kipling understood that Lodges needed a warrant from the United Grand Lodge of England to be regular Lodges (see Chapter Four), but there is no clear evidence of where he derived the idea of the informal and unwarranted Lodge.

In The Interests of the Brethren is a story which has very little action, other than a brief introduction of the characters followed by a Lodge meeting. The narrator becomes acquainted with Brother Burges, who takes him to a Lodge meeting. He describes the events of that meeting and the ceremony followed by the festive board and the story ends. It is, however, an unqualified tribute to Freemasonry and its ability to lift men in difficult times. It is the first occasion that we meet these damaged and shell-shocked servicemen but as Professor Tompkins observes it "is free from the notes of bitterness and apprehension that strike across those written in the subsequent peace."[9]

Kipling, in a letter held in the Grand Lodge Library in London, wrote to a Brother Fluke who had made contact to thank him for the story. In his reply Kipling says "I am afraid it was rather presumption on my part to have written it, as I have never passed the Chair and have held no rank higher than that of Secretary, but, like yourself, I have heard visiting Brethren during the War express their keen satisfaction wherever they found 'a cosy corner among the Brethren' at Lodge." He signs the letter "Yours fraternally Rudyard Kipling MM."[10] The implication of this comment may be that Kipling did visit lodges, especially during the First World War, but there is not a single scrap of evidence to corroborate that, with the single exception mentioned earlier. Nonetheless the story exudes a warm feeling of fraternity that will register with any Freemason.

Like many of Kipling's stories this one starts with an accidental meeting- in this case the narrator meets a stranger in a bird shop who advises him which canary to buy. They meet again by chance a few months later on a railway station platform and he has a moment to thank the stranger for his advice on the canary, before the stranger disappears into the crowd.[11]

Years later the narrator goes into a tobacconist shop to sort out a problem with his pipe (Kipling himself was an avid smoker), and the man behind the counter immediately asks after the canary. Such is Kipling's skill, that he conveys all these three meetings within a few short sentences. The narrator of the story, assumed to be a Freemason (although he is never specifically asked) is finally introduced to Lewis Holroyd Burges, the tobacco shop owner. Burges, it turns out, is a Freemason and has lost a son in the War (also called Lewis).[12] There is more than a little of Kipling in Burges, though Kipling very rarely mentioned his son in his writings after the war.

Burges complains that his pre-war hobbies, canaries and fishing, have lost their appeal since the death of his son in the war. While he attends to the narrator's pipe, a soldier enters the shop and Burges speaks to him in an undertone, and the soldier departs. Burges tells the narrator "Many of my clients are soldiers nowadays, and a number of 'em belong to the Craft." He bemoans the fact that the soldiers have no palate for tobacco. He rebukes the narrator for mistreating his pipe. "It deserves better treatment than it's had. There's a procedure, a ritual in all things."

The narrator leaves the shop thinking that he might have made a friend, and only a few yards on is approached by a wounded soldier, who asks direction to Burges's shop. By the time of his third visit to the shop he has learnt far more about Burges and his business interests. Although he runs the tobacco shop (in his family since 1827) he also has an interest in a major cigar importer. "I'm a shopkeeper by instinct," said Burges. "I like the ritual of handling things." This is the constant theme - ritual - Masonic and non-Masonic. Hardly a page of the story is written without reference to this love of ritual. Kipling makes very little concession to the non-Masonic reader, to whom much of this story must seem somewhat arcane. The more perceptive non-Masonic reader will have appreciated that it is the emphasis on ritual as a form of catharsis that is key to the story.

With his relationship established with Burges, the narrator becomes a regular visitor to the shop. On one visit a wounded Canadian soldier enters the shop, enquiring baldly whether he is in the right place. Burges asks who sent him. The soldier replies, "A man from Messines. But *that* ain't the point! I've got no certificates, nor papers- nothin' you understand. I left my Lodge owin' seventeen dollars back-dues. But this man at Messines told me it wouldn't make any odds with you." Burges responds by assuring the soldier that it doesn't matter and tells him when the Lodge meets, warning him that he will have to be proved. The soldier limps off happily and the narrator asks Burges who he was. "I don't know any more than you do- except he must be a Brother. London's full of Masons now. We must do what we can these days. If you'll come to tea this evening, I'll take you on to Lodge afterwards. It's a Lodge of Instruction."

Thus the reader and narrator are introduced to the Lodge Faith and Works No.5837, meeting on the third Saturday every month, with the Lodge of Instruction meeting every Thursday "but we sit oftener than that because there are so many Visiting Brothers in town." One would expect to find evidence of such Lodge meetings in the Grand Lodge archives, but none exists. This is unusual for Kipling, as so often many of his stories have their roots or origin in either his own experiences or events that he had encountered.[13]

Incidentally, currently there is a real Lodge with the number No. 5837. It is called Middlesex Century and meets at Uxbridge in Middlesex, but it was not formed until 1941 - some 24 years after Kipling wrote about the fictional Lodge. When Kipling wrote his story in 1917, there were less than 3800 Lodges in existence under the authority of the Grand Lodge of England. The years 1918 to 1939 were busy years for British Freemasonry, and over 2000 new Lodges were consecrated during that period. Growth was also caused by the consecration of new Lodges after each World War, as returning servicemen often used Freemasonry to preserve the camaraderie they had enjoyed during the preceding conflict.

It is an anomaly that Kipling gave this Lodge a number. He clearly understood from the content of the story that it was an unofficial and unwarranted Lodge. Therefore it could not have a warrant or a number. Lodge names and numbers go together and Kipling may have felt that he had to give his fictional Lodge a number for verisimilitude. Perhaps he chose this number knowing that it could not be confused with an existing Lodge.

So, finally, they leave for the meeting and again the theme recurs. "Yes, we owe that much to the Craft", says

Burges referring to the fact that he has dressed up smartly. "All Ritual is fortifying. Ritual's a natural necessity for mankind. The more things are upset, the more they fly to it. I abhor slovenly Ritual anywhere." This point could hardly get greater emphasis from Kipling.

It has been assumed, since the first mention of Freemasonry in the story, that the narrator is a Mason, and before they depart for Lodge, Burges recruits him to help examine the visiting Brethren. The narrator himself is never examined. Mrs. Burges hands her husband his initialed apron case as they depart. Burges warns his companion that he must not be too critical of their Lodge premises, which had once been a garage. In fact they enter "a carefully decorated ante-room hung around with Masonic prints." Whether Kipling remembered these from years earlier, when his father had helped him decorate the Masonic Hall in Lahore, or whether he had recently researched it, his list of the hangings is impressive. He refers to prints showing Peter Gilkes (1765-1833) a London greengrocer who, with Barton Wilson, was a founder of the Emulation Lodge of Instruction and was the father of Emulation ritual. The walls also display Kneller's portrait of Christopher Wren, Dunkerley and several other prints of Grand Masters including Anthony Sayer, the first Grand Master in 1717.

What follows might be part of any evening at any Lodge meeting. The narrator is introduced to the stalwarts of the Lodge, including Brother Leeming, and he is shown more prints. Kipling describes the fittings and appointments of the Lodge room, "...every detail was perfect in particular kind and general design." Even the ashlars are made from the best Carrara marble and, despite

Burges' protestations, it is apparent that the furniture of the Lodge is quite valuable.

Burges and Leeming describe how they collected some of furniture of the Lodge, but the discussion is cut short as it is time to go to the examination room, where a few men in uniform are waiting to be proved. There are some old confessional boxes left over from a church which they use to examine the brethren in privacy. Burges warns the Narrator not to be surprised by what he will find. He meets a Scotsman with part of his face blown away, who cannot speak properly but made the correct signs, and a New Zealander with only one arm and that in a sling. One soldier, whose Masonic credentials the narrator distrusts, turns out to be a Past District Grand Officer. Of the last brother that he examines, Kipling says "Everything seemed to have gone from him." The brother can't remember anything but swears that he is a Mason. This again provides a strong clue to Kipling's own views on Masonry. The soldier pleads with the narrator, "I wouldn't pass my own self on my answers, but I give yer my word that so far as I've had any religion, it's been all the religion I've had. For God's sake, let me sit in Lodge again, Brother!" This is expressed so forcefully by Kipling that one cannot but speculate that it represents his own view, and it is all the more surprising that he never resumed an active involvement in Freemasonry. It also confirms Kipling as a passionate advocate for the Craft.

After every visiting Brother has been examined, aprons are distributed. Some of the Brethren are quite emotional-including a "shell-shocker". Kipling describes at least fifty Brethren parading into the Lodge, including ten or twelve who are crippled and need assistance. The Brethren exchange small talk. For the non-Masonic reader, Kipling lets the narrator explain that, as a Lodge of Instruction, the Lodge is limited to rehearsals and lectures and cannot confer Masonic degrees. Brother Burges takes the Chair, welcomes the Brethren and asks them what ceremony they would like to perform and which Lodge offices they would like to take. When the visitors show reluctance to assume these duties and claim lack of practice, Burges reminds them why they are present. The real therapy for the visitors will lie in their attempt to perform the ceremony.

When a visiting organist is unable, through his injuries, to mount the steps to the organ loft, they carry him up. The visitors are persuaded to take the various offices in the ceremony to be rehearsed, and to do all the work. The regular members are forbidden to prompt, and the visitors do the work of the Lodge, but badly. We are not told the nature of the ceremony. A member of the Lodge asks a visitor at the end of the ceremony, "D'you like it?" The visitor replies, "Do I? It's Heaven to me, sittin' in Lodge again. I haven't much religion, but all I had I learnt in Lodge." Kipling has blurred the line here. For Kipling, who had detached himself from formal religion for some years, is perhaps using Freemasonry to fill a gap in his life. If he is trying to establish it as an alternative or quasi-religion, this is an approach that would be vigorously rejected by the Masonic authorities.

This visitor, who is a one footed RAMC corporal, continues enthusiastically "Yes, 'veiled in all'gory and illustrated in symbols'- the Fatherhood of God an' the Brotherhood of Man; an' what more in Hell *do* you want?" He comments on the ceremony "See! See! They've tied themselves in knots. I could ha' done it better myself- my one foot in France. Yes, I think they should do it again". It is clear that the Lodge Brethren thought it was better for the visitors to struggle and do the ritual rather than just be spectators. The therapy for the visitors was in attempting the ceremony. Having done that the visitors ask the Lodge Brethren to do it again-"they demanded an exhibition-working of their bungled ceremony...". For a man who had had virtually no active Masonic experience for nearly thirty years Kipling shows a remarkable feeling for the nuances of the Craft. The narrator says "Then I realized for the first time what word-and-gesture-perfect Ritual can be brought to mean." After that Burges delivers a short lecture on what sounds like a Tracing Board.

Then Kipling takes the story off in a totally unexpected direction. Burges asks the visitors how they would work part of the ceremony in their jurisdiction. One Brother offers a version from Jamaica; others join in from different parts of the world. Although they are still technically in a meeting, cigarettes are now distributed. Another Brother introduces Dutch ritual. Many current and active Freemasons would have a difficult task to equal the degree of knowledge displayed by Kipling in this story.

Brother Doctor Keede, a regular member of the Lodge, explains to the narrator how the Lodge was conceived. Burges had had lots of servicemen dropping into his shop and had realized that all they wanted was to have a Lodge where they could just drop in and relax. "A man's Lodge means more to him than people imagine." Leeming had passed the word around at the hospital and numbers had grown. In the previous two years it had grown so that they held two evening meetings and two afternoon meetings for Brethren who couldn't get evening leave. The narrator and Keede agree, that neither had understood what the Craft meant until the War. Is this the voice of Kipling speaking here? If so, the source of this inspiration remains a mystery. These stories, and many written around the same time, project a unique devotion to the Craft. Masonry has had many famous sons but only Mozart in *The Magic Flute* has perhaps created art about Freemasonry at this level. Tolstoy briefly touches it in *War and Peace,* but later seems to lose interest. Based on Kipling's own sources for his stories, there must have been some meeting or experience which inspired this piece.

The story is far from finished, although there is still not much action. The narrator learns that they have had attendances of up to 84 at their "banquets". Visitors are not allowed to contribute to the cost. It is clear that the senior members are all quite well-heeled. Keede explains that the furniture and jewels of the Lodge are kept in immaculate condition. Again Kipling uses the theme of curing. "Cured a shellshocker this spring by giving him our jewels to look after. He pretty well polished the number off 'em, but- it kept him from fighting Huns in his sleep." This concept is used again in other stories in this volume.

The Lodge meeting is closed with greetings from the visitors. A long list of exotic places from both the north and south hemispheres follow, including Africa, Canada, Australia and other parts of the Empire. The details of the list again confirm Kipling's knowledge of the range of Lodge names. Finally a silent Brother is desperately trying to give greetings. Somebody explains that he is giving greetings for a Lodge in South Wales. A hymn is sung followed by the Entered Apprentices' Song and the Brethren move into the banquet room.

Conversation over the Festive Board is sparked by a clergyman Brother, asserting that Masonry is an intellectual pursuit. Here Kipling puts up the proposition for another character to knock it down. He is rebutted by an Engineer officer, who relates the story (again the story within the story) of how a year earlier in Flanders, a dozen brethren had held a Lodge meeting in the ruins of a church, surrounded by stones (the rough ashlars) and no furniture. The clergyman thought that would be enough, "I warrant you weren't a bit the worse for that", said the Clergyman". "The idea should be enough without trappings." But he is told that they had made regalia out of camouflage and jewels from old metal.

This brings a rebuke from another Brother, "Ye were absolutely irregular an' unauthorized. Whaur was your Warrant?" When he suggests Grand Lodge ought to take action, another Brother interjects "If Grand Lodge had any sense, it 'ud warrant travelling Lodges at the front and attach first-class lecturers to 'em."

One brother asserts that Grand Lodge could reap huge revenues from authorizing such Lodges. An Engineer officer offers, "I could design a complete travelling Lodge outfit under forty pounds weight." Kipling would probably know that military Lodges, such as the ones he encountered in India, did have such compact travelling kits.

The debate continues vigorously. Even during the banquet, visiting Brethren arrive, some still carrying Flanders mud. They are given food. The clergyman watches over them as they fall asleep, so that he can make sure they catch their trains later in the night.

The narrator talks to other Brethren, admires the prints and the collection in the cases as the talk continues, and the meeting gradually begins to conclude. The remain' members contemplate what they could achieve, "We could do much with Masonry." says a Sergeant–Major.

"As an aid - as an aid - not as a substitute for religion," responds the clergyman. This quickly becomes contentious. The argument on Religion versus Freemasonry flares briefly, but Burges takes the discussion in another direction. "There ought to be a dozen-twenty-other Lodges in London every night; conferring degrees too, as well as instruction." Attention returns to the food and it turns out that the ham for the sandwiches is provided by Brother Leeming from his own pigs. Bro. Leeming's pigs will appear in other stories! The Clergyman rouses a sleeping soldier by tapping on his helmet, so that he can catch his train. The man jerks awake and puts his hand out for his missing rifle.

As the proceedings draw to a close, the narrator wonders "what would happen if Grand Lodge knew all about this". He tells Leeming, "It's all very nice, but it doesn't strike me somehow as regulation." From nowhere, it seems that Kipling has now appointed himself an authority on Masonic regulation. Leeming tells the narrator that they will settle it after the war. Burges adds the comment that, "There ought to be scores of them." His enthusiasm knows no bounds, "Think what could have been done *by* Masonry *through* Masonry *for* all the world". He thinks Grand Lodge has missed an opportunity, although some Brethren do seem genuinely concerned about the legality of what they have done. Leeming is afraid that the clergyman will inform on them.

As Burges and the narrator depart together, the narrator's final private thoughts come as a shock. "I said nothing. I was speculating how soon I could steal a march on the Clergyman and inform against 'Faith and Works'

No.5837 E.C." This is the surprising and brutal end to what has been an evening of Brotherly love and some emotion. The narrator, who has not uttered a hostile word throughout the meeting, indicates in the last line of the story that he might destroy the whole enterprise. None of Kipling's critics, Masonic or otherwise, have offered any explanation for this. Having pressed the value of ritual so highly and endorsed the form of meeting, this apparent contradiction is hard to comprehend. It is the only time that the legitimacy of the Lodge is questioned and the issue does not arise in any of the other Masonic stories.

Burges, who appears in several stories, feels strongly that freemasonry has curative properties for Brethren who have been in the War, but he also feels "that Grand Lodge may have thrown away its chance in the war almost as much as the Church has." The story is shot through with sympathy and support for the troops.

The story is quite astutely described by Sandra Kemp as "more like a narrative sketch of exhausted veterans seeking a reprieve from the pressures of war; a context which enables Kipling to expose Freemasonry as a possible technique of healing."[14] As Shamsul Islam describes it, "... for ritual after all is an imposition of order that leads to a greater order behind the chaos of material life."[15]

Looking at this story in isolation, no Freemason could fail to be moved by it, as it demonstrates all the human qualities that are exhibited by members of the craft. As a literary work, despite its slightly esoteric background, it illustrates Kipling's unrivalled mastery as a story teller and as a virtuoso of technical detail. In just twenty three pages he conjures up this self-contained world where we feel we could almost be processing into Lodge with these veterans and watching their ceremony.

The Madonna of the Trenches

Although *In the Interests of the Brethren* has much to engage Freemasons, it cannot compete with *The Madonna of the Trenches* as a dramatic story. This starts as another tale set within the framework of the Lodge room of Lodge of Faith and Works, yet it contains within that frame possibly Kipling's greatest love story, and at the same time it is an outstanding supernatural story. Other stories in the same collection, such as *The Wish House* and *The Gardener* contain a supernatural element (and also are love stories), but this story has received widespread acclamation even among some of his sternest critics. Lord Birkenhead said it was "the most brilliantly written."[16] Seymour-Smith complained about the Masonic setting as "an unworthy frame for what must be one of the supreme Ghost stories."[17] Perhaps the greatest plaudit comes from Professor Tompkins who defines this period of his work; "Now he shows himself more and more aware of the frailty of man's body and brains, his liability to manifold injury, his capacity for suffering and his fortitude in it." [18] It also demonstrates the range of the writer and that his Masonic-based stories have such immense diversity.

With Kipling's normal brevity, we learn very quickly that some Brethren at the Lodge are still seriously affected by their war-time experiences, and there is a doctor at hand in the Lodge to deal with any sudden emergencies. This story is clearly set post-bellum. Apart from obvious physical disabilities, several Brethren are suffering from shell-shock. The Senior Warden, Bro. Dr. Keede, has an important role. Keede had been a medical officer with a South London Battalion during the last two years of the War, and often knows the visiting Brethren. On this night he encounters a young newly-made Brother, Clem Strangewick, who had been a Headquarters Orderly in his old battalion, where the doctor had treated him for shell-shock. After the Lodge working, the Brethren then sit through what seems to the narrator to be a tedious lecture on King Solomon's Temple. During the lecture Strangewick becomes increasingly agitated and stumbles out of the room. The Brethren laugh, as they assume the tedium of the lecture has driven him out of the Lodge room.

Dr.Keede immediately follows him, and with the help of the anonymous narrator, ministers to Strangewick and takes him into the Tyler's room. The doctor pulls up a chair which creaks, and Strangewick becomes even more distressed at that sound, and at that point his war-time experiences in the trenches are disclosed.

Strangewick had spent time in the trenches in the winter, where everything was frozen, and that included dead bodies that were used to shore up the emplacements. This had been done by the French troops, who had used corpses to control the mud. Although there were duckboards along the bottom the trench, if the boards were missing, the soldiers ended up walking on the dead. Keede tries to convince Strangewick that this ghastly memory will recede. He gives him some medication.

At this point Keede recalls an incident in the frozen trenches that leads on to the real story. He recounts how an elderly Platoon Sergeant, about to go on leave, instead of taking the normal route out of the trenches to get himself to Arras and to leave in England, instead gets into a dug-out in the trench and settles down to warm himself between a couple of braziers burning charcoal. The Sergeant, John Godsoe, fails to see that the door only opens inwards and locks it. In the morning he is found frozen to death, gassed by the fumes of the braziers. Keede had seen the body the following morning, and had a slight suspicion that it might not have been an accident.

The last man to see him alive had been Bro. Strangewick. The doctor and his patient recall the investigation that followed the discovery of the body, and the disturbed state to which the incident reduced Strangewick. Keede is convinced that it was not the creaking corpses that affected the soldier, but something else that he has not admitted.

Then the full story is revealed. The young Bro. Strangewick had known Sergeant Godsoe all his life, and regarded him as an uncle, although he was not a blood relative. As he was over fifty years-old, Godsoe could have avoided military service, but he joined up and wanted his adopted nephew assigned to his platoon. From the front, Godsoe wrote to Strangewick's mother with news of her son and, as her eyesight was poor, the letters were read to her by her childless younger sister Auntie Armine, the stalwart of the family. Armine was the children's affectionate nickname for her. Her real name was Bella. As Strangewick was completing his last leave home, Auntie Armine asked if he would give a message to Godsoe."Well then, tell 'im from me", she says, "that I expect to be through with my little trouble by the twenty-first of next month, an' I'm dying to see him as soon as possible after that date." Auntie's "little trouble" was cancer (another sometime obsession of Kipling who suspected he might have it himself, and it appears in another story in the same collection).She wrote the message down for him, and he said goodbye.

Strangewick returns to the front, where he is employed as runner, taking messages along the trenches. On January 11th, three days after his return, he is given a message to take to a Corporal Grant, and at the same time he delivers his message to Godsoe. As he chats to Grant, the Corporal looks over at Godsoe studying his message and comments, "I don't like it." The men are uncomfortable with Grant, who claims to have Second Sight and his ability to prophesy the future. Strangewick rebukes Grant for his comments and nods at his "uncle" John, who pockets the note, saying, "This suits *me*. I'm for leaf on the twenty-first too."

Keede asks what happened next. Strangewick met his uncle periodically during the next ten days, and it was part of Strangewick's duties to remind the men going on leave, so that they could get to the station to catch the train on time. He describes his experiences that day, traversing the trenches during heavy bombardment. It is then that he notices the bodies under the duck boards.

It is also then that he sees something ahead of him-something "just like Auntie Armine waitin' beside the door...." He is amused when he discovers that it is only some old rags and a sandbag that has played a trick on his eyes. He continues with his duties to warn the leave takers, including his uncle. The German bombardment has made things chaotic. Later that evening he meets Uncle John, "scrapin' mud off himself, havin' shaved- quite the dandy." His uncle inquires about the Arras train. The two go down the trench together and John Godsoe asks Strangewick if he has any messages for home. Strangewick makes a joke of having thought he'd seen his Auntie in the trenches. Godsoe's response is "Oh-you've seen 'er, 'ave you?" Strangewick explains how the sight of the sandbags and some rags in the dark had deceived him.

They reach an awkward point in the trenches, where Clem Strangewick is reluctant to continue. Godsoe picks up a couple of braziers and tries to calm Strangewick's fears about this part of the trenches. Then Godsoe makes an odd speech, repeated in the story by Keede - part of the funeral service. "If, after the manner of men, I have fought with beasts at Ephesus, what advantageth it me if the dead rise not?"

The two men continue along the trench, frozen and creaking, Godsoe with the two braziers. As they approach an abandoned dressing station. Godsoe asks his nephew,"Where did you say she was, Clem? Me eyes ain't as good as they used to be."

"In 'er bed at 'ome," he replies. He then reports Godsoe as saying," "Why, Bella!"

Then Clem Strangewick continues "An' then I saw – I tell you I *saw* - Auntie Armine herself standin' by the old dressin'-station door where first I thought I'd seen her. He was lookin' at 'er and an' she was lookin' at him." He describes the way Godsoe and Bella look lovingly at each other. Godsoe tells her that it is only the second time they had been alone together in all the years. "You can shop me for a lunatic tomorrow," says Clem to Keede," but I saw it- I *saw* 'er answering to 'is spoken word!"

Godsoe continues his conversation with the apparition, then takes the braziers through the dug-out door, and lights them. Strangewick describes how Armine watched this, standing with her arms out. Godsoe invites her into the dug-out, and she goes in and Godsoe shuts and wedges the door shut. After this Clem Strangewick doesn't remember clearly what happens to him. He is woken in the morning to be told that Godsoe had not made the train. He is questioned about the events of that evening.

Later that day he encounters Grant, who tells him that he had found his Uncle John with the door shut and sandbags wedged into the cracks. Strangewick thinks the door had blown to, locking Godsoe in there, and he has suffocated from the fumes but Grant tells him that Godsoe has laid up a supply of a charcoal in anticipation of what he was going to do. Keede asks Strangewick whether Grant had known what Godsoe intended. Strangewick had carried on with his duties until he had a wire from his mother saying that Auntie Armine had died on the morning of the 21st. He reminds Keede that the doctor had lectured the troops about the Angel of Mons and hallucinations when they had been billeted in Arras.

"If the dead *do* rise - and I saw 'em - why - why *anything* can 'appen. Don't you understand?" Strangewick becomes increasingly agitated, and the Brethren are concerned about his mental state, as he rambles incoherently. Suddenly he quietens again, and Keede expresses his relief that he has got his problem off his chest. Strangewick continues to ramble about lawyers and suing. From the Lodge they find the Brother who had introduced Strangewick to the Lodge, and who is upset over the disturbance that has been caused. Keede tries to relieve the Brother's mind by taking the blame for raising the events of the War, but the Brother confides in Keede that Strangewick has another problem. Here there is a delicious Kiplingesque twist. In the last page of the story he throws in not one but three surprises. First, one cause of Strangewick's problems is that he is being sued for breach of promise. Secondly, the claim is made by the girl that he was courting while he was in the army, though since the incident in the trenches with his Uncle, he has rejected her.

Finally, as Keede advises Strangewick's host to let him sleep and take him home gently, he inquires the Brother's name. " 'Armine' " said the old gentleman. "He's my nephew by marriage." The elderly brother is puzzled by Keede's reaction to that information, but Keede just repeats the medical advice to keep the patient quiet.

Kipling may have had the idea for this story from the legend of the Angel of Mons, which became a popular rumour after the first major battle of the War. [19] The story that passed around was that a band of angels had protected British soldiers during the battle, and they were compared to the bowmen who had saved the English at the Battle of Agincourt. Few of the combatants in that 1914 battle survived the war to throw more light on this supernatural occurrence. More likely it was an apocryphal story, based on the writing of Arthur Machen, whose fictional short story about the Angel was taken up by the press, and the line between fact and fiction deliberately blurred.

The Janeites

This story is preceded by a poem:

Jane lies in Winchester-blessed be her shade!
Praise the Lord for making her, and her for all she made!
And while the stones of Winchester, or Milsom Street, remain,
Glory, love, and honour unto England's Jane!

The worship of Jane Austen became a major industry in the late nineteenth century. Austen may not divide critics as strongly as Kipling, but she still has her critics.

Some disparagers have claimed that her novels are mundane and dull, and just about girls seeking suitable husbands, while others have felt that she gave a much more accurate portrayal of life in the early part of the century, even if confined to the middle and landed classes. Austen has been accused by her detractors of ignoring national and global events happening around her (such as the Napoleonic Wars), and just concentrating on the minutiae of life among the country gentry.

Kipling was an ardent fan of Jane Austen, and her home city of Winchester was a place of pilgrimage for him. Her books were read aloud by members of the Kipling family. Kipling did not invent the expression "Janeites", but his name is more closely associated with that name than any other writer. A Janeite is defined in the Oxford Dictionary as "an admirer of Jane Austen's novels" and the term was invented by the literary critic George Saintbury, who was a friend and admirer of Kipling, and also a respected academic and critic and noted expert on wine.[20] According to biographer Andrew Lycett, Kipling met Saintsbury during a visit to Bath and they discussed "the sense of fellowship felt by people who shared a powerful joint experience – whether fighting in war, or membership of a Mason's Lodge, even familiarity with the works of an author such as Austen".[21] It seems this meeting inspired Kipling and led to the birth of this story.

The impact that this remarkable story has made is illustrated by the fact that as recently as 2002 acclaimed thriller writer Nicholas Freeling used Kipling's *Janeites* to entitle his own novel *The Janeites*. (see later) He explored an identical concept to Kipling, namely that reading the works of Jane Austen is a natural therapy for those who are sick or despondent. The difference is that Kipling places his story within a quasi-Masonic lodge, combining the therapy and comfort gained by the servicemen in the Lodge with the benefits of reading Austen. Another modern novel published in 2004 is *The Jane Austen Book Club* by Karen Joy Fowler, again taking Jane Austen's books as a therapy to bind a group of people together.

Critics were not universally pleased by Kipling's story. C.S.Lewis, in a talk printed in the Kipling Journal, called it "the hardly forgiveable Janeites", feeling Kipling had needlessly exploited Jane Austen to create another set of insiders. [22]

This is a harsh interpretation, and Lycett's analysis, which suggests that Kipling was looking for something that created a sense of companionship and community, is a preferable explanation.

Kipling, in his homage to Jane, created a strange and enigmatic story. The difference with this story compared to other tales in *Debits and Credits*, is that he combines his admiration for Jane with giving his sense of humour a freer rein – a rare occurrence at this time. One Kipling biographer says it is "a cunningly contrived story written with as many skins as an onion".[23] It is much deeper and more multifaceted than *In the Interests of the Brethren*. Kipling again employs the fictional Lodge of Faith & Works No. 5837, with a Lodge of Instruction as the setting, with Brother Burges at the helm.

Although Burges is common to these two stories, they are distinct in style. The former is a straightforward and uncomplicated story with very little narrative other than a Lodge meeting and the dialogue that precedes it. *The Janeites* is again set in that Lodge, but this merely provides the framework for the war story within it and again includes a Brother's unusual war-time experiences.

It also has a touch of Cockney and *Barrack Room Ballads* humour and despite the traumas of the War, shows Kipling at his most imaginative.

This story, set in 1920, starts with a detailed description of the Lodge furniture- vitally important to the members as every item has a symbolic meaning. As the Brethren clean and polish the Lodge's possessions during their regular Saturday afternoon clean-up, they discuss the war. Visitors are welcome to join in this process. In return for their contribution towards the cleaning they also get light refreshments. Burges, described as a Past Master, has them cleaning everything in the Lodge room including the hangings and curtains and the Pavement. They also polish the columns, jewels, the working "outfit" (presumably tools) and the organ. The narrator is given the Officer's Jewels which are made of Georgian silver. The pavement, which is of stone, has been cleaned so well it is described as a "glassy as the aisle of Greenwich Chapel."

Another brother tells Burges how the Emblems of Mortality should appear following the custom of his Mother Lodge. The narrator comments that he has never seen spit and polish to touch it. It is hard to see contemporary Masons doing much of this work.

Burges reminds the narrator that he should wait until he sees the organ, where Brother Anthony, a taxi-driver whom the narrator had met at a previous meeting, is in charge of cleaning. The cleaning is part of the post-war healing process provided by the Lodge and a chance for them to get some companionship. Burges points out Bro. Humberstall to the narrator. Humberstall, now a hairdresser, had been blown up twice during the War, while he was in the Artillery. The narrator asks Burges whether Humberstall had been affected by his war time experiences. Burges's cryptic response is, "Not much more than Lazarus did, I expect."

The narrator joins Humberstall with Bro. Anthony in cleaning the lodge organ. Humberstall is described as "an enormous, flat-faced man, carrying the shoulders, ribs and loins of the old Mark '14 Royal Garrison Artillery, and the eyes of a bewildered retriever...". It seems Humberstall had been in the middle of telling a story to Anthony, about a man called Macklin.

Humberstall describes how he returned to his unit for active service after having been invalided out. As he had been blown up before being invalided out, he was exempt from front-line service and had been given light duties in the officers' mess. Macklin had been given the task of showing Humberstall his duties as a mess waiter. Humberstall thought that this role was a bit demeaning, but there was no vacancy for him in his former position as a gunner. He describes Macklin as "a toff by birth; but that never showed till he was bosko absoluto". Macklin's breeding only came out when he was totally drunk. Bro. Anthony asks Humberstall what made him go back to the front at all. He had obviously been fed up at home, with his mother being distressed about the progress of the war. He hadn't been expected back at his unit, and as they hadn't an immediate position for him on the guns, his officer, Major Hammick, told him that until a casualty occurred he would have to work as a mess waiter.

He then describes the two officers – Hammick, who, in civilian life was a divorce lawyer, and Captain Mosse, who ran a Detective Agency. "Wives watched while you wait, an' so on". The two officers had not met until the War. They spent a lot of their time at the front, discussing their seedy divorce cases - which sound unattractive and grubby.

Humberstall says that when they had finished discussing matrimonial matters, they went on about "this Secret Society woman I was tellin' you of – this Jane. She was the only woman I ever 'eard 'em say a good word for". Initially he didn't take much interest, but then a new Lieutenant joined the Mess, who, in civilian life was an actuary. At first Hammick and Mosse ignore the new arrival, but when he hears them mention Jane, the Lieutenant, nicknamed Gander, pricks up his ears. A password is exchanged and immediately Gander is admitted to "the Society" and the port passed back.

Humberstall then describes to the brethren the ensuing conversation between the officers. He hears Hammick bemoaning the fact that Jane Austen died childless. Mosse responds, disputing that "I maintain she was fruitful in the 'ighest sense of the word." Gander supports Hammick in this argument but accepts "...she's left no direct an' lawful prog'ny." Humberstall hadn't been watching Macklin and has not appreciated until that moment that he is totally drunk.

Macklin, committing what must have been an awful gaffe for a mess-waiter, crudely interrupts the officers' conversation to correct them "Pa-hardon me, gents", Macklin says "She did leave lawful issue in the shape o' one son; and 'is name was' Enery James". Gander immediately challenges Macklin to prove his case. Macklin delivers a long lecture lasting fifteen minutes, reinforcing his claim. Humberstall listens to all this, and can even measure the time it takes by listening to the number of guns firing nearby. At the end of his tirade, Macklin falls flat on his face – "bosko absolute!" Kipling must have been chuckling when he wrote this. Henry James, whom he makes Jane Austen's "son", was of course one of the greatest writers of his generation, and close friend of Kipling, and one of the few witnesses at his wedding.

The officers put Macklin's outburst down to shell shock, and Humberstall is instructed to remove his colleague's unconscious body. Humberstall tells his listeners that that incident put into his head the idea of becoming a Janeite himself. He says he would have had the same idea, even if Macklin had been "a 'igh-up Mason." Questioned by the brethren about that comment, he says, " 'E'd never gone beyond the Blue Degrees, 'e told me". He recounts how Macklin, using his "toff's voice", had lectured his superior officers. Kipling replying to an invitation to a Lodge, used that same phrase in a letter informing the Lodge Secretary that he had "never been beyond the Blue Degrees."

The following day, Humberstall had pressed a now sober Macklin to explain how this new degree was worked. Macklin retorted that Humberstall was not fit to be initiated into the Society of the Janeites. Poor Humberstall, who is not the brightest soldier, does not grasp that Macklin is only using this as a pretext to extract cash from him.

And Macklin is easily bought. He has already extracted "fifteen bob" (75p) from Humberstall and puts up his price for information about Jane to a "Bradbury" (a pound - John Bradbury was the Secretary to the Treasury whose signature appeared on the bank notes), and for that amount he tells Humberstall the Pass-Word of the First Degree, which is *Tilniz an' trap-doors*. Humberstall's request for an explanation of *Tilniz* is fobbed off. "You obey orders," 'e says' "an' next time I ask you what you're thinkin' you'll answer, *Tilniz an' trap-doors* in a smart and soldierly manner," retorts Macklin.

Later that day, during the officers' lunch, Macklin tests Humberstall on the password, and is overheard by Captain Mosse, whose reaction is to take a dozen Turkish cigarettes out of his cigarette case and leave them on the table for the waiters to divide between them. Macklin reminds Humberstall what a good deal he is getting for his Bradbury. The latter is not convinced, feeling that there must be a lot more to this Janeite business. Macklin immediately offers to instruct him in the "'Igher Degrees among the Janeites, includin' the Charges, for another Bradbury...."

Bro. Anthony suggests that he was being a bit generous with his money, but Humberstall's reaction to that was that their life expectancy on the front averaged about six weeks. He also confirms that he didn't regret his decision, although it was a tough preparation. "In the first place, I come under Macklin for direct instruction *re* Jane."

Macklin is smugly satisfied, but Humberstall is worried in case they try and prove him, and he might need other passwords. "There must be a lot more to this Janeite game". In exchange for another Bradbury, Macklin offers "all the 'Igher Degrees among the Janeites, includin' the charges....".

As they clean the Lodge furniture, the incredulous Brother then questions Humberstall about Jane and whether she is real. Since the war Humberstall had read her entire works but found them dull. Much of Humberstall's experience is described in the conversation that follows. Humberstall's touching naivety adds humour to their conversation. To Humberstall "Jane? Why she was a little old maid 'oo'd written 'alf a dozen books about a hundred years ago". His colleague in Lodge, a taxi-driver, goes off at a tangent to describe an argument with a passenger that day where the two discover they have served in the same arena of the War and found much in common. That digression brings the conversation back to Jane and another speech by Humberstall on the works of Jane. "I mean 'er characters were no use! They was only just like people you run across any day".

He compares some of the characters in the books to people he has met- including his family. Bro. Anthony asks if he had discovered what *Tilniz* meant. "Yes, 'e was a swine of a Major-General, retired and on the make. They're all on the make, in a quiet way, in Jane." The Cockney conversation continues about Jane. Kipling, as well read as any of his contemporaries, knew his Jane Austen well and in using Sir Henry Tilney, a character in *Northanger Abbey*, is emphasizing the stupidity of Humberstall. Sir Henry made the famous statement in the novel, "The person, be it gentleman or lady, who has not pleasure in a good novel, must be intolerably stupid". Aloud, and on the stage, it would be hilarious, but the delicious irony seems to have by - passed many Kipling devotees.

Humberstall relates that he was in Jane's home town of Winchester, invalided there with trench foot. (Kipling had been a recent visitor to Winchester). Macklin describes it as holy ground, but Humberstall retorts, "My feet tingled right enough, but not on account of Jane". He then relates another incident at the front where it was practice to give the large ten-inch guns a name, but when the Janeites chalked *Reverend Collins*, *General Tilney* and *Catherine De Burgh* on individual guns they got into trouble and, as the mess-waiters were non-combatants, they were breaking the unwritten rules. The lawyer Hammick had held an impromptu hearing and the mess-waiters got off with a warning after the Battery Sergeant Major was placated with port.

As they polish the Lodge jewels, Humberstall explains what later happened to his unit. They were having a short break from the front line when they came under bombardment, and they were ordered to retreat. All members of the unit were killed in the ensuing bombardment and Humberstall was the only Janeite to survive. He is convinced he owes his survival to Jane.

Burges calls the Lodge from labour to refreshment. The Brethren quietly talk about poor Humberstall, "He's apt to miss 'is gears sometime", which is the after-effects of his second blowing up in the War. His mother or sister come to the Lodge to take him home. They speculate about the Jane story and whether the Janeites were an invention by the poor man, but dismiss that possibility.

The Janeites is another Kipling story that has divided his critics. Some think it is a wonderful homage to the great Jane, but others like Philip Mason feels it cheapens her and treats her "as though she were a popular barmaid."[24]

After the story, Kipling included in the same volume a poem entitled *Jane's Marriage* as further homage to Jane Austen. The first stanza reads

Jane went to Paradise:
That was only fair.
Good Sir Walter met her first,
And led her up the stair.
Henry and Tobias,
And Miguel of Spain,
Stood with Shakespeare at the top
To Welcome Jane-

The poem ends with Jane's marriage in Heaven. At the end of the story, which adds this comic element to tragedy, Humberstall, now restored to civilian life and his hairdressing shop, looks back on the experience and concludes, "I read all her six books now for pleasure 'tween times in the shop; an' it brings it all back - down to the smell of the glue-paint on the screens. You can take it from me Brethren, there's no one to touch Jane when you're in a tight place. Gawd bless 'er, whoever she was."

Nicholas Freeling's *The Janeites*, mentioned earlier, is not a run of the mill detective story.[25] The writing is economical and sparse in a way that Kipling would have been quick to commend. One leading character is a slightly eccentric French cancer specialist who, apart from being a Jesuit, recommends the novels of Jane Austen as a therapy to a patient and vows to turn him into a Janeite. He calls it "The Humberstall Effect". The patient, a recently retired senior government security officer, has the novels read to him as part of his treatment. Kipling's story is retold by the doctor. Throughout the story, references are made to the Kipling story, and the qualities of soldiers in the original are demonstrated by Freeling's characters.

A Friend of the Family

This story is also in the volume *Debits and Credits,* but was first published in Maclean's Magazine in June 1924. Again the setting is the Lodge Faith and Works No. 5837, English Constitution. This time the story starts at the end of a Lodge meeting, when the Brethren have carried out three initiations and two raisings. That is a mighty programme for a regular Lodge, never mind an unofficial one. Kipling does not try to explain how an unauthorized Lodge can do that, and it seems to contradict what he wrote in earlier stories, where the lodge was only for instruction. The Brethren sit down to enjoy sandwiches, pork pies and conversation. One Brother is from Australia, and Kipling, as usual, cannot resist a topical allusion. The Aussie, Orton, had served at Gallipoli and is ribbed about the possibility of his country becoming a republic (still under discussion nearly 90 years later!) and that is linked to a joke about the Tichborne claimant.[26] Another Brother, Bevin, had lost half his battalion at Gallipoli. Orton complains "They gambled us away in two days." After the banquet, Orton, Bevin and a third Brother, called Pole, settle down to chat. The Australian is full of anger against the British over the failures and casualties at Gallipoli, and a heated exchange of views takes place between them.

This is a prelude to the story, and the narrator in this case is Bro. Bevin, who is a chicken farmer from Chalfont St Giles. He starts by saying he would hate to have an Australian with a grudge against him. He tells an anecdote about an Australian called Hickmer or Hickmot (no-one in the story seems sure of his name), a young sheep drover from the remotest part of Queensland, who before joining up had lived his entire life in the outback among sheep and aborigines. He is described as never having seen a dozen white men together, until he joined up. After Gallipoli, with his regiment decimated, he had joined Bevin's outfit. Hickmot had the knack of being invisible. "He was the complete camouflager". He served in Bevin's platoon and was solitary and silent, except for the one single friend he made, a man called Bert Vigors - a friend of Bevin's from his home village. Vigors frequently airs his grievances about events at his village where, during Vigors' absence at the Front, a competitor, through unfair means, has damaged his family business and left him and his family impoverished.

Bert Vigors had quickly gained the nickname "The Grief". He was the only son of an elderly market gardener, and had tried hard to get exemption from military service to help his father, but had been turned down. To make matters worse, the same tribunal that rejected Vigors for exemption gave one to the newly established competition in his village, a man called Margetts. The result was that Vigors' family business went bust, and Margetts prospered. Bert was bitter about it, but Bevin, as his platoon sergeant, had tried to prevent him undermining morale with his unhappiness. Then Vigors met Hickmot, and a deep friendship was formed. They discussed little except sheep and Bert's grievance. Even as they waited to go over the top they talked of little else. In a break in hostilities, Hickmot made a model of Bert's village out of mud from the description Bert had given him. The Australian had a gift for carrying this picture in his head.

Then Hickmot was injured in December 1916, and a month later Bert Vigors was killed in action. The Australian lost a leg, and was invalided back to England. Bevin, by now, suffering from the effects of the war, was offered a post at home as a bombing instructor, went home and married Bert Vigor's sister. Bevin's listeners start to get impatient for the rest of the story about Hickmot.

Hickmot had been sent to Brighton, and then on to Roehampton, to get a new leg fitted. Bert's sister was anxious to meet her late brother's friend, and he spent time with the Vigors family and helped them on their smallholding while he waited "for initiation into his new leg." As ever, Hickmot was virtually invisible, and hardly spoke. After his stay Mrs. Bevin saw him off on the train to Roehampton.

The following morning in the early hours, Bevin was woken by an explosion. Aeroplanes were heard, followed by three big bangs. A little later, Bevin saw first one hay rick, then another, alight on the Margetts' property and a bomb hole in the roof of the Margetts' house. The Margetts' horses had been let loose and were busy grazing on their vegetable patch. The young Margetts had a broken arm. In daylight, the damage was inspected - the house, the hay ricks, the greenhouse and the new vegetables had all been destroyed. But, by some freak of fate, there was no other damage in the village- except one bomb had apparently landed in a field and created "inadvertently" a pond for the Bevins' ducks- a pond which had previously been refused by the local Estate owners.

The Australian's immediate response to this story: "And Hickmot?"

A subsequent enquiry by an explosives expert decided that "it was just a lucky shot on the part of one isolated Hun 'plane going home, an' we weren't to take it to heart." The expert decided it was new type of incendiary bomb. Bevin, of course, being an explosives instructor, knew the fuse of a Mills bomb when he saw it. He had no doubt that it was all done by Hickmot – the only question was how. He had obviously quietly purloined the bombs when he had visited Bevin, while he watched him instructing. He had then planned the subsequent destruction like a military operation, including giving young Margetts a broken arm.

A month later Bevins met Hickmot while on a visit to Brighton and told him how the bomb incident had unhinged Margetts, and enabled the Vigors to get back their business, and the ducks to enjoy their new pond. Hickmot didn't seem interested in any of this, and only wished to get back to the sheep and aborigines in Queensland with his new leg. As they say a final farewell to him, Bevin comments how grateful they are to the Germans for sorting out Margetts. Hickmot responds "Bert was my friend."

The brethren chuckle as they go out into the night.

This was not the only revenge story that Kipling wrote, and more often than not the neatness of the revenge appealed to his sense of justice. With his hatred of the Germans, Kipling occasionally strayed too far in the search for vengeance. *Mary Postgate* is perhaps the ultimate in revenge stories, though it has no Masonic element. [27]

Fairy-Kist

Although this story does not appear in *Debits and Credits,* it has been included here as it fits neatly with the other Masonic stories that Kipling wrote in the latter part of his career. It also contains characters common to the stories in *Debits and Credits.* The story was included in the volume entitled *Limits and Renewals,* published in 1927, which was Kipling's last collection.

Like most Kipling stories, it had been published earlier in a magazine. In *Fairy-Kist* we meet "The only important society in existence today" – the *Eclectic but Comprehensive Fraternity for the Perpetuation of Gratitude towards Lesser Lights.* [28] We also meet some of our old friends from the stories in *Debits and Credits,* and in particular Lewis Holroyd Burges who is the society's Secretary. It appears that this is just a dining club, whose object is to honour minor figures in the arts and sciences. The reference to "Lesser Lights", although taken from Freemasonry, is meant more as pun than a serious reference. The Fraternity has resemblances to a Masonic Lodge and its characters have all appeared in earlier stories involving the fictional Lodge, Faith and Works No. 5837, and the story is replete with Masonic allusions. It is also another example of Kipling inventing clubs or societies as he had done in South Africa during the Boer War.

As in the earlier Masonic stories, the Fraternity is used as setting for a tale within a tale. Kipling manages to combine a slightly tongue in cheek gesture to his fellow writer, Arthur Conan Doyle, by telling a detective story and within the same story, exhibiting his love and knowledge of gardening and even a reference to his newly rediscovered sport of golf. As well as the creator of Sherlock Holmes, Kipling also introduces popular contemporary children's author Juliana Horatio Ewing whose stories contribute to the narrative.

As the story starts, Robert Keede, the surgeon, offers to tell the members "a true detective yarn." The narrator (who tells the story in the first person and must be assumed to be Kipling himself) responds by saying that if the story is worth it, in return he will finish the task of cataloguing a mass of Masonic pamphlets (1831-59) bequeathed by a Brother to Lodge Faith and Works no. 5836 E.C. (note the error in the Lodge number – it should be 5837!). He admits it is a job he has shirked for months. This again is an interesting Kipling thought. What gave him the idea for the existence of such Masonic pamphlets? One shouldn't forget his membership of Quatuor Coronati and wonder whether he might have obtained some of his ideas from their publications.

The diners at the Fraternity are told the story of what had appeared to be a murder in the local village and how it was investigated. Suspicion had fallen upon a man who had suffered severely in the War, but the members of the Fraternity, playing detective, solved the mystery. The story darkens as the suspected murderer is a former soldier, who has suffered severely during the First World War. But the mysterious death is eventually explained to everyone's satisfaction. The "murder" turns out to be a freak accident. The shell-shocked war victim is completely innocent. The solution to the alleged crime would do credit to any of the modern forensic detectives in current television fiction. Again Kipling returned to his theme about men damaged in the conflict – in this case the victim had found solace and relief in his love of botany and gardening.

The fictional Lodge Faith & Hope was preserved in name as a real Craft Lodge with the same name but numbered 5079, founded in Wolverhampton in 1928. It exists to this day.

Kipling's later work in collections of stories such as *Debits and Credits* and *Limits and Renewals* did not receive the attention they merited during his lifetime, and it is only in the half century after his death that a serious reappraisal of these stories has led to their acceptance as some of the best of Kipling's output, and a very clear indication of the quality of the mature Kipling. Although the Masonic stories are central to several of these stories, it would be wrong to ignore some of the other stories in these volumes. Anyone picking up *Debit and Credits* would be denying themselves a rewarding experience by missing stories such as *The Gardener*.

CHAPTER SEVEN

KIPLING'S POEMS-
MASONIC AND OTHERS

It may surprise many contemporary readers that, before the First World War, Kipling was better known for his poetry than for his short stories and fiction. Leading literary critics have accepted that his poetry was more widely read than any poet since Chaucer and Shakespeare. His verse output was prodigious. Kipling's poems were eagerly taken up and published in national newspapers, and read by a large part of the population. His poem *If* is probably the most quoted poem in the English language, but it is only a tiny part of his oeuvre, and one of the few poems still well-known in its entirety today. He was probably the last poet to command a mass audience. [1] Yet Kipling wrote poetry in a wide range of styles. *If* may have been hammered into the head of many British schoolboys, but he wrote his early verses for the Anglo-Indian market. *Departmental Ditties*, published when Rudyard was barely twenty one, was hugely popular both in India and throughout the world.

Today he is remembered primarily as the author of memorable children's books and for some of his short stories, but he is entitled to much higher prominence for his poetry. Critics such as T.S.Eliot described his poems as mere verse but, it might be asked, whether there was some resentment and envy at Kipling's popularity. Also perhaps, Kipling poems rarely required a gathering of literary experts to interpret their meaning. In Kipling's heyday, poetry was something read by the man in the street. Modern poetry has become so remote from contemporary man that it is hard to imagine the impact made by some of Kipling's poems. They reflected the depth of his reading and wide general knowledge, often with Biblical references. The only poets in the last fifty years having some of the same appeal as Kipling are possibly John Betjeman, Dylan Thomas and Philip Larkin.

His popularity as a poet was cemented by his cockney ballads. These were written in the dialect of the ordinary soldier that he had met in India. They appealed equally to the service man, and the man in the street. He had already had great success, which started with *Departmental Ditties* published in 1886, and he followed that with the hugely successful *Barrack Room Ballads* in 1892. The latter contained some humorous verse, but others, like *Danny Deever*, were dramatic and serious. This is a poem which describes a young soldier facing execution for the murder of one of his fellows. It must rank as one of the most striking and moving in the English language. The poems, although written in the tongue of the ordinary soldier, never lack for depth or clarity and often, under the guise of humour, touched the heart of the ordinary man. That same volume included *Fuzzy Wuzzy*, where the British Tommy pays tribute to the courage and fighting skill of his enemy. *In*

The Widow at Windsor, as will be seen, Queen Victoria receives the Masonic treatment as an erstwhile Mother of Hiram, and the soldiers become the Widow's Sons. The same volume contained *Gunga Din*, and the immortal line "You're a better man than I am, Gunga Din!" and also *Mandalay*. These dialect poems often made ideal material for music hall songs. Today many people use lines taken from Kipling poems, without even knowing their origin. Kipling's poems deserve to be read aloud, and often single lines are quoted without any understanding of what the whole poem was meant to convey. If his early short stories had not put him in the public eye, then his poems would have done that for a different and often wider readership. Freemasonry features in many of his poems and it is a guide to his continued interest and regard for the Craft that the Masonic poems are such a significant element in his output. Even a modern Poet Laureate cannot attract a tiny proportion of the readership that Kipling regularly enjoyed. From his return to England in 1896, his poetry increasingly reflected major political and international issues of the day.

It has been suggested by many critics that he should have succeeded Tennyson as Poet Laureate, instead of the vastly inferior Alfred Austin. There has been speculation that Queen Victoria may have vetoed his appointment because she was offended by his poem *The Widow at Windsor*. There is no evidence to support this and, in fact, it was quite common for the Queen to be known by that affectionate title among her forces. Added to that is the fact that Kipling had been abroad for most of the period after Tennyson's death. There was a gap of six years before Austin was appointed and it is said that Kipling was "sounded out" for the appointment but was not interested.[2] That would certainly have been consistent with Kipling's general refusal to accept most honours that he was offered. Although he wrote poems to mark major events, such as the Diamond Jubilee, he also hated to write to order. Austin was a minor poet, and there were several other more worthy candidates, including Kipling's close friend Henley. Margaret Drabble describes Austin's poetry as "of little merit".[3] Kipling may also have been considered too young at that point in his career. There is certainly no evidence available that Kipling was ever formally rejected for the office. Some years later, when Austin died, in 1913, Kipling may not have been considered as his political sympathies, were, by that time, out of step with the then government, and he was perceived as a controversial figure. With his record of refusing most of the honours that were offered to him, it is unlikely that he would have been tempted, even if it was offered.

It is also questionable whether Queen Victoria would have understood the Masonic references in the poem which compares her to the mother of Hiram Abiff. The poem starts:

"'Ave you 'eard o' the Widow at Windsor
A hairy gold crown on 'er 'ead
She 'as ships on the foam-she 'as millions at 'ome
(An 'she pays us poor beggars in red!)"

The poem continues as music – hall doggerel, bemoaning the lot of the "poor beggars in red" and emphasizing the wealth and power of the Queen

"For the Kings must come down an' the Emperors frown,
When the Widow at Windsor says "Stop!".

It goes on to praise the Empire;

"Then 'ere's to the Lodge of the Widow
From the Pole to the Tropics it runs-
To the Lodge that we tile with the rank an' the file.

He maintains the analogy to the last verse, comparing the guarding of the Empire to the task of tiling a Masonic Lodge, and concludes:

Then 'ere's to the Sons of the Widow,
Wherever, 'owever they roam.
'Ere's all they desire, an' if they require
A speedy return to their 'ome.
(Poor beggars!- they'll never see 'home!)

This was rather a cynical finish, and diminishes the effect of the poem but it was nevertheless realistic, as so many soldiers perished overseas, especially in India. The last verse leaves no doubt as to where Kipling got the idea. Yet again he drew on his Masonic experiences. It is doubtful if many Lodge tylers know that Kipling used the words for their familiar closing toast. That last verse is found on many Masonic websites and some Lodges apparently use it as an alternative tyler's toast although they omit the last line.

In the volume *The Seven Seas* (1896), Kipling again devoted a poem to the Queen, but this time in a serious but rather jingoistic vein. In the *Song of the Dead* after toasting the Queen, he goes on to compare the British Empire to a Lodge:

When Drake went down to the Horn
And England was crowned thereby,
'Twixt seas unsailed and shores unhailed

Our Lodge-Our Lodge was born
(And England was crowned thereby!)

In the same volume he draws again on his Masonic knowledge in *The Merchantmen*;

"King Solomon drew the merchantmen
Because of his desire,
For peacocks, apes and ivory,
From Tarshish unto Tyre;
With Cedars out of Lebanon
Which Hiram rafted down,
But we be only sailormen
That use in London town."

One of the great attractions of Freemasonry in India was that it enabled Kipling to mix with a wider cross section of people. In his teens and early twenties Kipling sought new people and new experiences and his work as a journalist added to that on a daily basis. In the Lodges in Lahore, Hindus, Sikhs, Muslims, Parsees and Jews mixed with Christians and other religions or sects.

For his most popular Masonic poem, Kipling used the voice of an old soldier, reminiscing with his comrades at home, about his time in India. *The Mother Lodge* is a sentimental and affectionate recollection of a Lodge in India and possibly has some autobiographical elements, although the membership of Hope & Perseverance No. 782 does appear higher in the social order than the members of "my Mother Lodge". It is also a reflection of the life of the British officials who ran so much of the administration in India.

There was Rundle, Station Master,

An' Beazley of the Rail,
An' Ackman, Commissariat,
An' Donkin o' the Jail;
An' Blake, Conductor-Sergeant,
Our Master twice was 'e,
With 'im that kept the Europe-shop,
Old Framjee Eduljee.

Although this may not have reflected the reality of Kipling's own Lodge, membership of this idealized Lodge is further described, this time to introduce the Indian members. It emphasizes how normal divisions disappeared once they entered the Lodge:

Outside-"Sergeant! Sir! Salute! Salaam!"
Inside-"Brother, an' it does do no 'arm,
We met upon the Level an' we parted on the Square
An' I was Junior Deacon in my Mother Lodge out there!

We'd Bola Nath, Accountant,
An' Saul the Aden Jew,
An' Din Mohammed, Draughtsman
Of the Survey Office too;
There was Babu Chuckerbutty,
An' Amir Singh the Sikh,
An' Castro from the fittin-sheds,
The Roman Catholick!

Possibly Kipling had visited other Lodges which were more down to earth, for the Lodge described in the poem is obviously a poor one - probably the European members were ordinary soldiers, while Kipling's Lodge had a large number of senior army officers and the Indian Masons were quite distinguished. Kipling himself never reached the office of Junior Deacon.

We 'adn't good regalia,
An' Our Lodge was old an' bare,
But we knew the Ancient Landmarks,
An' we kep' 'em to a hair,
An' lookin' on it backwards
It often strikes me thus,
There ain't such things as infidels,
Excep' ,perhaps it's us.

For monthly, after Labour,
We'd all sit down and smoke
(We durst'nt give no banquets,
Lest a Brother's caste was broke)
An' man on man got talkin'
Religion an' the rest,
An' every man comparin'
Of the God 'e knew the best.

How different this seems from our modern prohibition about discussions on religion.

This again is consistent with Kipling's regard for ritual, which features so strongly in the stories in *Debits and Credits*. The verse quoted above describes how they could not hold a banquet because different religions might be offended by the food, but they did discuss religion. The Hindus would not eat beef, and the Jews and Muslims would not eat pork, so it was better to avoid food completely. Lodges did have some form of refreshment, but had to take religious differences into account. In the Handbook of the District Grand Lodge of the Punjab for 1888, the District Grand Master entreats the Brethren to keep the accounts for Lodge expenses separate from those for the banquet. He also recommends that Brethren should not be asked to subscribe for meals, which, for religious reasons, they could not partake. [4]

So man on man got talkin'
An' not a Brother stirred
Till mornin' waked the parrots
An' that dam' brain-fevered-bird;
We'd say 'twas 'ighly curious,
An' we'd all ride 'ome to bed,
With Mo'ammed, God, an' Shiva,
Changin' pickets in our 'head

It is possible that Kipling visited more lodges than we suspect while he was in India. We can be fairly certain he went to Mian Mir, and probably visited several times. We can also be fairly sure that he went to a Lodge in Calcutta, referred to in his letters and the possible source of the story for *The Man Who Would Be King*. The next verse widens the scope, and shows that Kipling still felt some strong feelings for what he had enjoyed in India:

Full oft on Guv'ment service
This rovin' foot 'ath pressed,
An' bore fraternal greetin's
To the Lodges East an' West,
Accordin' as commanded,
From Kohat to Singapore,
But I wish that I might see them
In my Mother Lodge once more!

The final two lines sum up the nostalgia:

We met upon the Level an' we parted on the Square,
An' I was Junior Deacon in my Mother Lodge out there!

In complete contrast, Kipling did not hesitate to use his verses to support his political views. He had started writing the pieces that became *Departmental Ditties* in 1885 during a summer break at Simla, and they were published in the *Civil and Military Gazette* between February and April 1886.They were published in four editions as *Departmental Ditties* over the next four years. T.S.Eliot, somewhat unkindly, dismisses them as clever verses but not poetry. Kipling's verses were not always profound or philosophical, but why should verse that is humorous or written in colloquial terms, be any less valid as art? It certainly found a huge market.

Kipling, the poet, who had left school at 16, had nevertheless become very well-read. However he rarely used obscure literary references or allusions from the classics. He wrote direct, clear and often controversial poetry, which left no-one in doubt about his sentiments. He used his verses, on occasion, to launch merciless attacks on those he hated or despised. Politicians were often the target, but on more than one occasion he used his poetry to raise large amounts of money for the troops. His poem *The Absent Minded Beggar*, published in the Daily Mail, raised £300,000 for soldiers' families during the Boer War. It was another reason that the forces became such admirers of the man.

His poem *Recessional*, regarded by some as a hymn to national unity, was first published in *The Times* in 1897. It was regarded as an outstanding public verse for an entire generation. It is described as "one of those rare poems that articulates a mood and moment in a nation's history". [5] In it Kipling, writing at the time of Queen Victoria's Golden Jubilee, tries to voice his concern that Britain is far too complacent about its place in the world. It contains a verse that we have already seen in Chapter 1 that still causes great controversy and arguments among Kipling interpreters.

If, drunk with sight of power, we loose
Wild tongues that have not Thee in awe,
Such boastings as the Gentiles use,
Or lesser breeds without the Law—
Lord God of Hosts, be with us yet,
Lest we forget,-lest we forget!

His reference to "lesser breeds" bought accusations of racism, but it is now generally accepted that Kipling was referring to the Germans. That one line has been more controversial than almost any other line that Kipling wrote. Kipling mercilessly attacked the Germans before both World Wars.

Most readers would consider *If* the defining Kipling poem. It is a call to manhood, to be strong in the face of adversity, and to take whatever life has to offer. Another lesser-known poem which might well be placed alongside it is *The Thousandth Man* which appeared in *Rewards and Fairies*. This poem starts with a statement from King Solomon, and is a simple tribute to that one defining friendship that every man would wish to enjoy. The sentiments that the poem expresses- standing by a friend whatever the circumstances, are in keeping with Freemasonry, but the only Masonic reference is in the first line:

One man in a thousand, Solomon says,

Will stick more close than a brother,
And it's worth while seeking him half of your days
If you find him before the other.
Nine hundred and ninety-nine depend
On what the world sees in you,
But the Thousandth Man will stand your friend
With the whole round world agin you.

The Palace, written in 1903, is contained in a volume of poetry entitled *The Five Nations*. By Kipling standards this poem is not easy to interpret. It has many Masonic overtones, but some of the references are quite obscure. The poem refers to building a palace on the ruins of an earlier one. The Masonic and building terminology used in the poem were familiar to Kipling. It is an allegory for Kipling's own work and his relationship with the world as an artist. But different writers have produced widely differing interpretations.

The poem commences:

When I was a King and a Mason-A Master proven and skilled-
I cleared me a ground for a palace such as King should build.
I decreed and dug down to my levels, Presently under the silt,
I came on the wreck of a palace such as a King had built.

There was no worth in the fashion-there was no wit in the plan-
Hither and thither, aimless, the ruined footings ran-
Masonry, brute, mishandled, but carven on every stone:
'After me cometh a Builder. Tell him; I too have known.'

Swift to my use in the trenches, where my well-planned ground-works grew,
I tumbled his quoins and his ashlars, and cut and reset them anew;
Lime I milled off the marble; burned it, slacked it and spread;
Taking and leaving at pleasure the gifts of the humble dead.

At the start you might think that this poem has links to the Royal Arch, although Kipling was never a member. However, that cannot explain the major part of this poem. In an interesting article about it on the Kipling Society website, George Kieffer comments that, although much of the symbolism and imagery is Masonic, it is not simply a Masonic poem but shows Kipling's knowledge of building and construction. The notes by Kieffer and Mary Hamer also contain the very pertinent comment, "Rejecting a community founded on Christianity, he had embraced the ideal of mutual respect and brotherhood he discovered among Freemasons".[6]

It was typical of Kipling's courtesy to correspondents that when a Brother wrote in 1903 to thank him for the poem, Kipling said, "it is always pleasant to hear from one of the craft when one's Masonic verses are appreciated."[7]

Banquet Night, as mentioned in Chapter Six, appeared in *Debits and Credits*. In the poem, King Solomon sends messages to Hiram King of Tyre and Hiram Abif inviting them and their brethren to come and dine. Kipling had, of course, visited Jerusalem, which must have made some parts of the Masonic ritual more vivid. We have seen elsewhere that he purchased stone from the quarries, which became gavels. He would have visualized what life was like for the workmen as they laboured to cut the stone and build the First Temple. The poem is also a tribute to the Masonic festive board.

To finish this chapter we have what some may consider the most philosophical of Kipling's Masonic poems – and a strange one for a relatively young man. *My New Cut Ashlar* is a paean of praise to a fundamental Masonic symbol, but also an early statement of faith by Kipling. The poem first appeared in a letter to William Henley.[8] Henley was one of Kipling's most enthusiastic early supporters on his return to England. He was an editor, critic and poet, and became editor of the *Scots Observer*. Henley shared Kipling's view of the Empire, and was an important member of the group of writers with whom Kipling associated during this period in England, including Edmund Gosse, Thomas Hardy, Henry James and Rider Haggard. The poem was written in 1890, when Kipling was still only 25 years old. In the letter to Henley, the poem is entitled *Twilight in the Abbey*, with the sub-title *The Prayer of the Mark Master Mason*.

In his letter to Henley, Kipling writes:

"Would you kindly let me know at your convenience if the following is rot or what. I can't make it out and I don't seem to have been drunk when I did it." He signs it as he signed many letters to friends "Ruddy". He then sets out the poem which, although bearing many similar phrases, contains a number of very distinct and different stanzas.

After setting out the poem, and also suggesting a separate stanza which might be the first verse, Kipling finishes with the comment, "You can have it if you like or send it back with curses. Frankly I don't know what to make of it. If it's good for aught use it this week and don't be wrath." Henley obviously thought it was good, as it was published in the *National Observer* on 6 December 1890.

The first stanza given below was missed by many earlier writers. The letter to Henley was not published until 1990.

Kipling throughout his life was a great re-writer. He constantly revised his own work, and this poem received that treatment so that it eventually emerged as *My New–Cut Ashlar*. It appeared at the very end of the collection of stories, Life's Handicaps. This volume (subtitled *Stories of Mine Own People*) contains a number of his most famous stories, including *The Courting of Dinah Shadd, On Greenhow Hill* and *The Mutiny of the Mavericks*. It also has that famous line on the title page, which Kipling ascribed to a native proverb, "I met a hundred men on the road to Delhi and they were all my brothers".

This poem, however, is not placed specifically with any story. After four hundred pages and twenty-seven stories, *My New Cut Ashlar* appears on the very last page of the book. It is headed L'Envoi, though that is not the title of the poem. Many writers have used what is the old French literary practice of adding a detached verse at the end of a literary composition, serving to convey its moral. Kipling used an Envoi on more than one occasion.

The poem in the book begins:

My new-cut ashlar takes the light
Where crimson blank the windows flare.
By my own work before the night,
Great Overseer, I make my prayer.

The extra verse, sent to Henley, that Kipling did not include in the original edition reads:

Wherefore before the face of men
Great Overseer, I bring my Mark,
Fair craft or foul. In mercy then
Will that I die not in the dark!

For the benefit of non-Masons, ashlars are small blocks of marble that sit on the pedestal of the desks of the Senior and Junior Wardens in a Lodge room. Not only do they represent stone that was used in the construction of King Solomon's Temple, but they also have symbolic meanings. The rough and uncut ashlar is laid in front of the Junior Warden in the Lodge room, and is a stone that has been quarried but not smoothed off. It is described as symbolically representing man in his "infant or primitive state, rough and unpolished as that stone, until, by the kind care and attention of his parents and guardians, in giving him a liberal and virtuous education, his mind is cultivated and he is thereby rendered a fit member of civilized society."[9]

In contrast the perfect ashlar which sits in front of the Senior Warden "represents a man in the decline of his years, after a regular well-spent life in acts of piety and virtue." The perfect ashlar is a stone ready to be incorporated in the building of the Temple.

Is this last verse a plea by Kipling to God to give his approval to Kipling's work? To produce a perfect ashlar would be the ambition of any craftsman and Kipling, more than most writers, regarded his work as a craft and one for which he claimed something equivalent to divine inspiration. A Mason would be very proud of his new cut ashlar if it passed inspection, and Kipling seems to be seeking that approval. Kipling's biographer Charles Carrington links this poem to the world renowned *Recessional*, as representing Kipling's message throughout his life. "The impulse and circumstance of his own life were important only in relation to the Law, that temple built to the design of the Great Overseer." [10] Here the biographer adopts the Masonic terminology. Just as the Craft Mason describes the deity as the Great Architect, the Mark Mason uses the nomenclature of the Great Overseer.

CHAPTER EIGHT

OTHER MASONIC REFERENCES IN KIPLING'S WORK

When you survey the whole of Kipling's writings, both fictional and factual, the number of Masonic references is extensive. With his retentive memory, just as he found Biblical language came easily, he frequently used a word, phrase or expression that he had absorbed from Masonic ritual. Many references have not been generally recognized, as most non-Masonic writers have not always spotted when Kipling slips into the language of Masonic ritual. These words are found scattered in his stories, poems and speeches, as well as the use of Freemasonry as a benchmark for the conduct or behaviour of characters. At times, he simply selects a Masonic expression that succinctly reflects a particular sentiment. He is rarely self-conscious about it; to anyone other than Freemasons it might either go unnoticed or be accepted as another original piece of Kiplingesque expression or a reflection of his immense gift for language. The frequency with which the language of the Craft appears underlines his liking of Masonry, and more often than not the words he chooses underline his own quest for a moral barometer. With his wonderful memory he would have made a fine ritualist if he had remained active in the craft.

The examples given are by no means inclusive, and there are many that may well have escaped this writer and others who have read extensively through Kipling's huge output. Some of the references are more tenuous than others, and some are included as they are so close to parts of Masonic ritual with which all Freemasons are familiar. I have chosen the most significant ones, but students of Kipling will find many articles in the Kipling Journal that list other minor references. It would be equally difficult to list all the Biblical allusions in Kipling's work, of which there are many, and the real point might well become submerged in the detail.

The Day's Work

This volume, published in 1898, contains the story *.007,* subtitled *The Story of An American Loco.* Whether the number 007 was later purloined by Ian Fleming for James Bond remains a matter of conjecture. Kipling was fascinated by mechanical contrivances, including trains, ships and cars, and this is one of a number of stories featuring engines of various types. He reportedly spent many hours talking to the Stationmaster at Brattleboro station in Vermont to learn as much as he could about railways and trains. The story is primarily intended for children but, like any Kipling story, adults will still derive much from it.

In this story .007 is a brand-new locomotive, struggling to be accepted by the old locomotives in the engine sheds, and in the first part of the story .007 endures the relative hostility demonstrated towards a newcomer.

Eventually he is dispatched on his first major trip and, although beset by problems, he successfully completes his mission. On his return to the shed he is introduced to the leading locomotive, the Purple Emperor who pulls the express train. He is told by another engine, "He's the Master of the Lodge". The locomotive making the introduction continues, "This is a new brother, worshipful sir, with most of his mileage ahead of him but, so far as a serving-brother can, I'll answer for him".

The Purple Emperor responds, "By virtue of the authority vested in me as Head of the Road, I hereby declare and pronounce .007 a full and accepted Brother of the Amalgamated Brotherhood of Locomotives, and as such entitled to all shop, switch, track, tank and round-house privileges throughout my jurisdiction, in the Degree of Superior Flier, it bein' well known and credibly reported to me that our Brother has covered forty-one miles in thirty-nine and a half minutes on an errand of mercy to the afflicted. At a convenient time, I myself will communicate to you the Song and Signal of this Degree whereby you may be recognized in the darkest night. Take your stall, newly-entered Brother among Locomotives!" The story ends happily and it could be almost a fairy tale of Hans Christian Anderson proportions (like the ultimate acceptance of the Ugly Duckling), although one wonders what the listening children and their parents made of the Masonic ritual. With this story you could almost create a junior Freemasonry!

Professor Pinney, in an introduction to a modern reprint of these stories, makes the point, " It is commonplace in the discussion of Kipling that his stories present, over and over again, the values of duty, discipline, craft and self-sacrifice, a combination all subsumed in the single idea of work." [1] To Kipling the acceptance of the new engine and its membership of the group were based on the quality and commitment of its work, and the need to earn respect; this is a regular theme in Kipling.

Captains Courageous.

Kipling wrote this novel (first published in 1907) while he was living in New England, and he travelled with his close friend Dr. Conlan to meet the fishermen who got their livelihood from the Grand Banks. The story is quite simple and unadorned, although like anything Kipling wrote, the technical background to the fishing industry had been fully researched. The main character, Harvey Cheyne, is a cocky and spoilt fifteen-year-old travelling to Europe on a liner with his wealthy father, and making himself thoroughly unpopular with his fellow passengers. Shortly after leaving the United States, Harvey falls overboard and is miraculously rescued from the sea by a fishing boat named *We're Here*, which had only just set out on a long fishing trip. The captain, who is a tough disciplinarian, puts Harvey to work. The arrogant boy faces real authority for the first time in his life. He rebels at first, but eventually goes through an epiphany and by the time he is reunited with his parents some weeks later, he is an upstanding and reformed young man. This again is a story of how hard work and dedication are the best way to redemption, and Kipling inserts one Masonic incident.

In a crowded fishing area, Harvey and the crew encounter a French fishing boat. After a friendly exchange in pidgin English, the crew discover that Harvey speaks French and can ask the Frenchmen whether they have any tobacco to spare. Tobacco is bartered for chocolate, but Harvey found his schoolboy French was of no real use. On return to his boat he asks his fellow crewman Platt,

"'How was it my French didn't go, and your sign-talk did?' Harvey demanded when the barter had been distributed among the *We're Heres.*"

"'Sign talk!' Platt guffawed. 'Well, yes, 'twas sign-talk, but a heap older'n your French, Harve. Them French boats are chock-full o' Freemasons, an' that's why.' "

"Are you a Freemason, then?"

"'Looks that way, don't it?' said the man-o'-war's man, stuffing his pipe; and Harvey had another mystery of the deep sea to brood upon."

This exchange is the sole Masonic element in the entire book and why Kipling chose to insert it is difficult to explain. It adds little or nothing to the narrative but, as will be apparent, Kipling employed these small Masonic episodes in many stories. For such a careful and fastidious writer, this was not done unconsciously. In the end, as in so many Kipling stories, the initially arrogant Harvey earns respect by learning to work, and by the end of the story, he is returned to his grieving parents as a model young man.

The Captive

This is in one of Kipling's Boer War stories contained in the volume *Traffic and Discoveries*, published in 1902. He writes a tale of an American who has invented an early form of machine gun, and has taken it to South Africa to test it under war conditions. In the story, the leading character in *The Captive* is given some magazines to read by another character, including a periodical called the American Tyler. His excitement at receiving this establishes both parties' Masonic credentials, and an appropriate handshake follows. There is no other Masonic reference in the story but this one incident links the characters and establishes their relationship.

As described in Chapter One, Kipling devised a quasi-Masonic ritual while working in South Africa during the Boer War. Although that ritual was preserved it never had any practical application, but in 1922 he did devise another ritual using his Masonic knowledge for a ceremony that is still in constant use over 85 years later. Kipling wrote *The Ritual of Calling an Engineer* at the request of his Canadian friend H.E.T.Haultain. This ceremonial is still used for engineering students graduating from seven Canadian universities and can also be used for any professionally qualified Canadian engineer. It is called the Kipling Ritual and its components are unmistakably Masonic. The procedure is administered by a body named The Corporation of the Seven Wardens.

Each newly graduating engineer is required to take the Obligation at a graduation ceremony, and following that he receives an Iron Ring which is placed on the little finger of his working hand. The Obligation is private, though apparently not secret, but candidates are asked not to discuss it with others. The ring, which is made of rough iron, was thought to be intended to rub against drawings and paper upon which the engineer writes. (Shades of Masonic working tools!) Kipling suggested that the iron should be as rough as "the mind of the young." Kipling himself received one of the rings, which he warmly acknowledged.[2] His plans for the ceremony were contained in an eight page document which now belongs to the Corporation of the Seven Wardens, Custodians and Administrators of the Ritual of the Calling of an Engineer, in Montreal. To show how significant this remains in Canada, their Post office issued a special stamp in 2000 to commemorate the 75th Anniversary of the Ritual. The Ritual also includes the Kipling poem *The Sons of Martha*, which some think has Masonic connections although it would seem to be directly derived from the New Testament.

The Press

This poem was Kipling's view of the profession of which he had once been an active member. Even before the incident at Brattleboro, Kipling seems to have started to develop an aversion to the press. To evoke some of what he considered their unending insensitivity the poem starts:

The Soldier may forget his sword,
The sailorman the sea
The Mason may forget the Word
And the Priest his litany;

The Maid may forget both jewel and gem,
And the bride her wedding-dress—
But the Jew shall forget Jerusalem
Ere we forget the Press!

For someone who had learnt his craft as a journalist, and continued to derive benefits from the attentions of leading newspapers, he had no particular liking for the fifth estate. He spurned opportunities for interviews. Although the affair with his brother-in-law Beatty at

Brattleboro may have cemented his view about the press, even before that he had shown some irritation with their attentions. It is perhaps fortunate that he did not have to cope with the present-day tabloids.

On the City Wall

This story was first published in 1888, in the same month as *The Man Who Would Be King*. The story is based around Lalun, a member of the world's oldest profession. Her home on the City wall is a salon which attracts a wide range of visitors, including Shiahs, Sufis, Hindus, Sikhs and some very superior and influential people. One of her young lovers, Wali Dad, a twenty-two year old Muslim, is besotted with Lalun. He describes her situation to the narrator, "It is Lalun's salon.. and it is eclectic- is that not the word? Outside of a Freemasons' Lodge I have never seen such gatherings. There I dined once with a Jew- A Yahoudi!"

This short Masonic reference tells us several things. It was written by Kipling when he was a similar age to Wali Dad. There is no doubt Kipling enjoyed his nocturnal ramblings around Lahore and learnt much from them (which was the view of biographer Charles Carrington).[3] Whether he gave in to the temptations of a Lalun we shall never know, but he would not be the first young man to do so. However it is Wali Dad's comment on the Freemasons' Lodge that is so telling. At his Lodge, it would have been one of the first occasions when Kipling would have shared an evening with different races and religions - so far divorced from the very English atmosphere of the Punjab Club. It is noted that he makes reference to Wali Dad having met a Jew in his Lodge. The Tyler in Kipling's poem *The Mother Lodge* is also described as being Jewish.

Kipling is regarded by some writers as being anti-semitic. He did write material that could be considered so, for example the poem *Gehazi* which was a strident assault on Rufus Isaacs but he was not consistent. T.S.Eliot, accused of the same offence, acquitted Kipling of the charge and wrote that he was "not aware that Rudyard Kipling cherished any particularly anti-semitic feelings."[4]

The Bold Prentice

This is another story which illustrates Kipling's interest in technical knowledge of railways, this time setting his story in the Indian Railway system. The hero, Young Ottley, is an apprentice, who comes under the influence of Olaf Swanson, a Swede who runs the Government Mail Train. Swanson's importance is shown not only by that, but the fact that he is author of a manual on repairing locomotives, and also Past Master of the Railway Masonic Lodge, St. Duncan's in the East. Unlike the other half-hearted apprentices, Young Ottley is immersed in locomotive engineering, under the tutelage of Swanson. The benefit for him is that when he travels as a train passenger, and the locomotive blows up, Ottley comes to the rescue. From what he has learnt from Swanson's tuition, he is able to direct the repair operation. Swanson witnesses his triumph, and shortly afterwards Ottley receives rapid promotion and becomes a driver. The reference to Swanson's Lodge is the only Masonic link in this story. According to the Kipling Society's notes [5] on the story it is believed that the Lodge referred to was St. George's in the East No. 1526. Again Kipling has indicated that mastery of one's craft is the key to character.

With the Main Guard

This story (see Chapter Four), one of Kipling's earliest, appeared in the first volume of the *Indian Railway Library* in 1888. As Kipling describes it in his Preface to the first edition, "...further adventures of my esteemed friends and sometimes allies, Privates Mulvaney, Otheris and Learoyd....". The story is not only a wonderful description of a military skirmish (which one suspects Kipling got from the horse's mouth), but in using the words from the Third Degree in Freemasonry, it seems totally appropriate in describing how the comradeship between the soldiers was also their salvation.

The Dog Hervey

Masonic references appear in Kipling's work in the most unexpected places. *The Dog Hervey,* which was published in 1914, appeared in the collection *A Diversity of Creatures.* It is an odd story about a very strange dog with a serious squint, called Harvey, who appears to a character called Shend in a hallucination, while he is suffering the effects of malaria. His companion, the narrator, recognizes the dog that Shend describes. To test whether his companion can really see the same vision, Shend asks him to describe what the dog is doing. "I'll letter or halve it with you. There! Begin." The two characters then do exactly that, spelling out the eight-letter word which describes the dog's distinctive action by alternate letters. It is another example of Kipling not wasting anything he learnt from his days as a Freemason, in this case it is the Masonic habit of spelling secret words letter by letter rather than pronouncing them in full. It is the only Masonic allusion in this story.

Rout of the White Hussars has been referred to earlier in Chapter Four where a nearby Lodge's skeleton used in its Third Degree ceremony, is purloined as part of a revenge plot to teach their officious commanding officer a lesson.

CHAPTER NINE

OTHER WRITERS VIEWS ON KIPLING'S MASONRY

As will already be apparent, critics and biographers have never been short of opinions on Kipling's work and character. Although he has been the subject of many major biographies and innumerable literary analyses, few of his biographers or critics seem to have made any real in-depth attempt to explain his attraction to the Craft. Some have made an intelligent guess at what attracted Kipling to it, but others have been guilty of wild and unsubstantiated speculation that must severely undermine their credibility and the quality of their research. Not a single one of his later biographers appears to have investigated what Freemasonry means in practice, to understand how it operates, what it might offer to its members, or how it contributed to Kipling's ideas and narratives. A significant exception to this is Sir George McMunn, who had not only served in India and been a prominent Freemason there, but was also a leading light in the Kipling Society. He displayed a real understanding of what the Craft meant to Kipling. For those interested in debating the reasons for Kipling's attraction to Freemasonry, this chapter looks at the wide range of opinions his interest has provoked. Some of those opinions are valid, but others will possibly provoke derision or scorn.

It should be acknowledged that Kipling's influence in the world went far beyond that of most successful authors. Somerset Maugham said, "His influence was great on his fellow writers, but perhaps greater on those of his fellow men who lived in one way or another the sort of life he dealt with. When one traveled in the East, it was astonishing how often one came across men who had modeled themselves on the creatures of his invention."[1] He continues, "He not only created characters; he moulded men."

His first official biographer was Lord Birkenhead, who was initially approved by Kipling's daughter Elsie Bambridge. She later angrily withdrew her agreement to the work, after a disagreement with Birkenhead over the content. His book was published, in 1978, by his son Robin after the death of his father and then of Mrs. Bambridge. Most subsequent biographers have assumed, (without any hard evidence), that she thought Birkenhead was too critical of her father. He had signed a contract with her that gave her virtually an absolute veto. Reading it now, the worst one can say is that it was perhaps a little too blunt in places for an elderly lady reading about her sometimes controversial father. There are no embarrassing revelations, or skeletons. Her second choice of biographer was Charles Carrington. It was only these two writers who had access to the Kipling family's own archives. The two biographers had vastly different views on Kipling's Masonic interest. They were both experienced writers, though neither had strong literary credentials and their strength was in understanding Kipling's period and his contemporaries, many of whom they interviewed.

Birkenhead claims that there are a number of aspects of Kipling's work that jarred on readers. He writes, "It is not surprising that Kipling became an ardent Mason. The strong instinct for being "inside", or "belonging" pervades his work from beginning to end....".[2] This claim of being "an insider" is a much repeated allegation. Kipling certainly had an immense thirst for knowledge and technical detail. Curiosity may well have been the initial spur which led him to join Freemasonry, but nowhere is there any suggestion that he exploited being a member of the Craft, or that the "secrets" gave him any advantages. He never boasted about his membership. Does being a Freemason make you an "insider"? I think most Freemasons would not consider themselves insiders – any more than being a member of a golf club, a Rotary club or any other social organization would make one such. Kipling's lack of involvement in Masonry after he left India suggests that that was not his reason for joining. This repeated claim about Kipling wanting to be an "insider" would seem an oversimplification.

Firstly, Kipling enjoyed the company of his male contemporaries. He was very much a child of the Victorian period in that respect. He had grown up in India, where the Punjab Club and the Officers' Mess provided a large part of his social life. He relished the company of military and naval men. As a younger man, he had several female friends but, once married, his friendships were very much male orientated. Secondly, he did not enjoy the literary society in London. He preferred the company of practical down-to-earth people like servicemen and railway drivers in preference to academics and intellectuals. He did, however, absorb all the new technologies of the 1890s and early twentieth century. He liked to be in the know about how machines worked.

Carrington, generally a reliable biographer, goes wildly overboard on the subject of his interest in the Craft. He describes Freemasonry as "one of the channels by which he (Kipling) penetrated the underworld."[3] He feels it was "a system that gratifies both his craving for a world religion and his devotion to the secret bond that unites 'the Sons of Martha'. These are extravagant claims. His attempted link from Freemasonry to the Sons of Martha is questionable. Did Kipling seek a world religion? I think more realistic argument is that Kipling, like many who have suffered personal tragedies, sought to find some way of rationalizing these events. If he had been more actively involved in Freemasonry he would have appreciated that Freemasons may consider they have a moral and ethical code, but do not want that to be confused with any form of organized religion. After the First World War it is arguable that he was looking for an answer to reconcile the losses he had suffered, especially the loss of John, and these boundaries became blurred.

Carrington is somewhat less cryptic with his other explanation. He sees Kipling as using Masonry because "it provided an underlying fellowship of humanity to shield the individual (and himself) from a constant nagging anxiety about his ultimate fate." [4] This may be a more balanced judgement and nearer the position of the mature Kipling, who clearly spent his later years in trying to find a philosophy for life. This is apparent from his conversations with Rider Haggard. However it would certainly not apply to the young Kipling. Overall,

Carrington's assessment is not a convincing one. As a journalist, Kipling had certainly explored the underworld of Lahore, but when one examines the membership of his Lodge it is highly representative of the hierarchy of Lahore society.

Since his death, Kipling has attracted more critical consideration than many other writers and more biographies than any other British writer apart from the Bard of Avon. This is a strange irony, as by the time of his death Kipling's standing had already been in serious decline with the literary establishment and even to some extent with the reading public. This may be linked with the relative lack of tributes on his death, though news of his demise was overshadowed by the death of King George V. Some critics had ignored most of his work in the last twenty-five years of his life. By the time of his death, literature had already moved on, and was becoming dominated by modernist writers like James Joyce, D.H.Lawrence and Virginia Woolf. However, the more percipient critics, a few years after his death, started to reappraise his later work and began to convince the sceptics that they had made a serious error in dismissing the later Kipling. Some of the recent appraisals of his late work also suggest that his influence on the generation of writers, including the modernists who succeeded him, has been underestimated. Although his last few collections of stories, like the earlier ones, could be inconsistent, there still remain some of the finest short stories. Many of those stories benefitted from his Masonic knowledge.

An early critical appraisal after his death was written in 1945 by American writer Hilton Brown. [5] It was done with some minor assistance from Kipling's sister Alice (Trix) Fleming. It is indicative of the relative fall in

Kipling's reputation that the book leaves no doubt that one of its principal objects is to revive critical interest in Kipling, and restore his reputation. Brown is scathing about the muted response to the death of the great man and the lack of eulogies. Whereas many critics considered Kipling "written out" by the 1920's, Brown dismisses this argument. In fact he selects two of the Masonic stories to illustrate his point. He recommends that the detractors should read *Debits and Credits* and he points to *The Janeites* and *A Madonna of the Trenches* as outstanding examples of the Kipling art. Brown, like many later writers, bemoans the "tantalizing" limitations of *Something of Myself* and the fact that it ignores most of the major events in Kipling's life.[6]

Brown also tackles the claim that Kipling always wanted to be an insider. Brown quotes the baggage master at Brattleboro, who said Kipling wanted to know everything about everything, and "he never forgot what you told him." [7] He continues, "But - to penetrate behind the veil, to subscribe to the tabu (sic), to exchange the secret password when fingers were laid upon the lips-therein, it seemed to Kipling, lay the delight of delights and the consummation of wisdom." Brown, guilty of somewhat overblown prose, presses on, " All through his life he yearned, with a persistence that survived more than one disappointment, to join some sort of Society, to be Initiate, to be a Member. That he became a Freemason as early as possible goes without saying: he could not *not* have been a Mason."[8] Like Carrington he has drawn rather unsubstantiated conclusions. First, in all probability, Kipling was invited to join the Lodge by a friend or acquaintance (as he himself makes clear because the Lodge needed a Secretary) and, secondly, until he joined it he would have known little or nothing about the Craft. But Brown is not finished yet. He notes that, for all his endless allusions to it, Kipling did not pursue the Craft into its higher stages and "that being initiated was enough, the knowing of the words, the sharing of the esoteric secrets". [9] Again the emphasis is on knowing the words, which is hardly the essence of Freemasonry. Brown draws a completely unjustified conclusion. Kipling certainly knew the significance of the words, as *The Janeites* demonstrates, although in that later story he used Jane Austen's names in a quasi-Masonic context, in homage to Jane, and in a humorous way. Earlier Kipling had used Masonic secrets more for dramatic effect than any other reason. In *The Man who Would be King* they are the key to Dravot and Carnehan convincing the natives of their powers and in *Kim* his Masonic documents are the key that unlocks Kim's true identity. However, all the writers who latch on to Kipling's supposed love of secrecy, ignore the fundamentals of Freemasonry – brotherly love, relief and truth.

Against Brown's argument it can be said that Kipling refused membership of several exclusive "clubs" which he was invited to join. He politely rejected the offer of a Knighthood on more than one occasion. He also declined the approach to become a member of the Order of Merit. He might even have become Poet Laureate, had taken a more popular line in some of the views he expressed publicly. Kipling did enjoy some aspects of his celebrity, and it brought him into contact with major figures all around the world. He received many honours, from the Nobel Prize in Literature, to honorary doctorates, but none of these rewards made him an "insider".

Where Brown may have been nearer the real truth is when he describes how Kipling developed his theory of "the Law". He considers that Kipling felt that man's ultimate objective should be to "perform his allotted task and perform it efficiently"[10] and that was the only way he could relate himself to the Universe. This is very close to the direction in the Third Degree, "Continue to perform your allotted task while it is still day ".[11] This is very much the essence of Kipling.

Another example of how Kipling divides critics is indicated in a book of essays on him edited by Professor Andrew Rutherford,[12] where eleven prominent academics and writers display a wide range of differing views on aspects of Kipling's character and work. Space here allows me to include only a small selection, and that does not include Kingsley Amis, Max Beerbohm, Robert Graves and many others who all had strong views on Kipling.

In the Rutherford collection there is an obituary lecture given by Professor W.L.Renwick who, very soon after Kipling's death, picked up the Masonic link.[13] He talks about how Kipling "understood and appreciated, thus, the morality of the tradesman, insisting that a man's job is a thing to be done for its own sake, with his strength, knowledge and conscience; and he saw that the business of everyman, soldier, engineer, administrator, or writer, is to turn out a clean finished job." This is entirely in keeping with the respect that Freemasonry gives to the honest craftsman.[14] His reservation is that Kipling could overdo the technical part – i.e talking shop, whatever form that would take. He adds," Kipling was an ardent Freemason, and at times he seems to regard the world as an aggregation of secret and semi-secret societies, a pattern of circles, intersecting indeed, but closed - English public schools, religions, engine-rooms, messes, nationalities, clubs, services and professions." This again would seem to be a simplistic conclusion and to say very little more about Kipling. Surely everyone's existence is made up of such circles? It would be more accurate to say that Kipling had a voracious appetite for knowledge, and if he displayed an interest in any subject he would not be satisfied until he had mastered it.

It is also an exaggeration to describe him as an "ardent" Freemason. The word suggests a degree of participation that never happened. If he had wanted to be an insider to the extent suggested by some of these critics, he would certainly have joined and attended Lodges and progressed in the Craft. One could argue that the opposite is true of Kipling. In many ways he appears a rather solitary figure rather than a constant joiner of groups. Continuing with the Masonic analogy, Renwick says, "Kipling was apt to despise the Lodges which chance or temperament or personal antagonism tyled against him." [15] This is another unsupportable generalization. Kipling held strong views on political and military matters, but this description of him ascribes to him attitudes that suggest that he deliberately attacked those who disagreed with him. He could express his opinions vigorously, even intemperately, but this comment also demonstrates how Masonic terminology can be misused.

In the same volume, there is an essay by leading literary critic Lionel Trilling, first published in 1943, in which he wrote [16] " ' Craft' and 'Craftily' were words that Kipling loved (no doubt they were connected with his deep Masonic attachment), and when he used them he intended all their several meanings at once- shrewdness, a special technique, a special *secret* technique communicated by some master of it, and the bond that one user of technique would naturally have with another." It is interesting that Trilling told the Editor Andrew Rutherford some years later that, if he had written that opinion later, he would not have been so censorious.[17]

A better assessment of Kipling, in the same collection, comes from George Shepperson, who considers the accusation against Kipling that he was a racist.[18] Shepperson starts with the obvious point that, in the nineteenth century, considerations of colour were poles apart from contemporary views. He feels that Kipling was capable of "profound imaginative sympathy and understanding for Indians of many kinds, and in Freemasonry he glimpsed the possibility of a brotherhood transcending the barriers of race, class and religion." [19]

In the same volume an essay by another academic Noel Annan addresses Kipling's interest in Masonry as a healing ritual. He recognizes that Kipling realized that many men break under the stress that society places on them. [20]

Sir George McMunn has a special place in the list of Kipling critics. As mentioned earlier he was a military man with service experience in India and a prominent Freemason. Of the impact of Freemasonry in the British Empire he wrote, "it is, perhaps, the greatest support that religion, morality and order have however little we suspect it."[21] Of its impact on Kipling he added, "Not only the historicity, the romance and tradition appealed to him, but also the universality of the science…". He continued, "The fact that it also works its secrets, its lessons and its ceremonies through a stately ritual, unwritten and handed down through the ages, at once appealed to his literary instincts, and to his ear, apt for effective phrases." That is a sentiment that few other Kipling critics have picked up. Kipling with his great love and knowledge of words must have relished the poetry of Masonic ritual. Much of Masonic ritual was inherited from prose written in the late Middle Ages and absorbed and adapted by the early Speculative Freemasons in the eighteenth and nineteenth centuries.

Another volume of excellent essays was edited by John Gross, and it is to his great credit that there is little overlap with the Rutherford collection. [22] One essay in this collection, by John Raymond, focuses on Kipling's final phase of writing and the influence that Freemasonry exerted on it. He first describes the work that Kipling did on the two-volume history of *The Irish Guards* and feels that the research on that factual work, and his relationship with his closest friend Rider Haggard, had much to do with the creation of the Masonic stories in *Debits and Credits*. In his research he had talked to many young soldiers who had fought in the First World War, listening to their terrible experiences. Raymond feels that the other element was his long discussions with Haggard, who was possibly one of the few to whom he unburdened his heart.

Perhaps the most controversial biographer is Martin Seymour-Smith, whose 1989 critical biography of Kipling outraged academics and admirers alike. Seymour-Smith makes clear that his approach is not the 'non-psychological' one of the authorized biographer Charles Carrington, but a more sophisticated one that attempts to show Kipling warts and all - a man who could be deeply humane but equally capable of a repulsive ideology that embraced racism. Where, however, he aroused the most indignation was his suggestion that Kipling had homosexual desires.

In his introduction to a later edition of his book the author dismisses his critics for a simplistic approach to his work and having a lack of understanding of Victorian sexuality. [23] Seymour-Smith has no doubt about Kipling's unqualified anti-semitism, which he categories as both absurd and repugnant, but does not claim that Kipling actually practiced homosexuality; rather he implies that he harboured dark thoughts about men. [24] On Freemasonry Seymour–Smith is dismissive of the Masonic element in the late stories.

He writes of *A Madonna of the Trenches*, "some small time is wasted in the Masonic business which serves as an unworthy frame for what must be one of the supreme ghost stories." [25] This comment demonstrates a lack of understanding of Kipling's approach for two reasons. Firstly, the whole purpose of the story is to demonstrate that the medium of the Lodge is the source of comfort to the narrator, who has endured this supernatural experience. Secondly, it is a fundamental to the Kipling technique to offer the tale within a tale and it is a technique that he uses to great effect.

Yet another biographer, Philip Mason, perceives that Kipling had a profound belief in ritual, "the performance as a discipline of certain acts which are socially acceptable and which have also a symbolic significance. Masonic rituals appealed to him; keeping things clean and bright; the craftsman's care of his tools; what he called 'soul-cleansing routine.'[26] Possibly Kipling was slightly influenced by his friend Thomas Hardy, whose characters frequently seem overwhelmed by the indifference of nature. Kipling, who frequently appears to feel the same way, sees an escape in ritual from the ever present malevolence of life to conscientious work and routine.

Sandra Kemp, looking at the late stories, quite rightly finds "Kipling first turning to the 'magic' and 'ritual' of Freemasonry to find the restorative balance he seeks."[27] She also notes that in the story *In the Presence* he had written of the precise ritual observance by Sikhs and Ghurkhas.

It is hard to draw any simple and straightforward conclusions from these diverse opinions. Kipling differs from many writers as he did not regard himself as a literary person. In the Modernist sense, he was not interested in the new psychology and character analysis that was transforming modern literature through the work of writers like Woolf and Joyce.

Andrew Lycett considers that Kipling was attracted by Freemasonry "to strike a better balance between his outer and inner selves-between his professional advancement and emotional development....." [28] Is this a thought that would be in the mind a twenty year-old? His subsequent comment carries more authority. "With its ideals of brotherhood, goodwill and charity, Masonry played an important part in bridging social divisions, both within the British community, and between Anglo-Indians and local people." He is the only biographer who seems to have researched the background of Masonry in the Punjab in this period. Lycett describes Kipling's involvement in Lodge Hope and Perseverance No.782 and why it was so important to him. "The reason was that Masonry, with its ethical and metaphysical elements, provided the nearest equivalent to a coherent belief system for a young man who, for all his knowingness, was still floundering to make sense of India's mass of conflicting creeds."

Having read possibly approaching two hundred critics and academics on Kipling, one conclusion is that his sheer elusiveness frustrates many of them. In an attempt to show they have the definitive view on him, many are deliberately provocative. Kipling himself hated that type of dissection and introspection, and felt that his fame did not require him to open his heart to all and sundry. He made it quite clear that he wanted his work to be judged on its own merits, without any consideration of his character and background. His autobiography *Something of Myself* further frustrated critics, as it did no more than hint at what might have influenced critical moments of his life. It made no reference to the great tragedies that blighted his life and it was, in some ways, clearly cryptic. Research into his life was not helped by the fact that, after his death, Caroline destroyed large quantities of his papers. Perhaps the best background is provided by Professor Pinney's six volumes of correspondence. Kipling was a prolific letter writer and fortunately many of his letters have been saved by the recipients.

Some critics have suggested that his attitude towards analysis of his work was because he felt his lack of formal education, and that he could not compete with those who had the benefit of a university education. Professor Pinney, in his introduction to *The Day's Work,* examined Kipling's concept of work and its connection to Freemasonry. He says, "This may remind us that Kipling as a young man at work in India had joined the Masonic Order, whose rituals and symbols both came from the craft of the stonemason-builder, supplying a ready-made language to express the values of work, initiation and community." [29]

Charles Carrington's authorized biography remains a major account of Kipling's life, although written more than fifty years ago. More recently the 1989 biography by Andrew Lycett provided a major reassessment of his life and had the benefit of half a century of additional research. Lycett is particularly convincing in his analysis of Kipling's interest in Freemasonry.[30]

Of the most recent biographies Jad Adams' *Kipling* published in 2005 is light but fresh, and eminently readable. It contrasts with many earlier biographies as this is more of a "no holds barred" approach. However he still makes the elementary mistake of saying that Kipling was invited to join Freemasonry by dispensation in 1885 because he was under 19. In fact Kipling could not have been under 19 as he had celebrated his nineteenth birthday in 1884. Still demonstrating some lack of research he continues, "The Masons also satisfied Kipling's need for a sense of religion which was not dogmatic, and provided him with a reliable set of contacts in every country he was to visit in his many travels in the future."[31] In fact, there is negligible evidence to suggest that Kipling used any Masonic contacts for more than the first year or so after leaving India, in early 1889. It is probable he used one or two on that first trip across the United States, but never thereafter. When he left India, in 1889, it was the first time he had been out of the sub-continent as an adult, and any Masonic contacts he had made would have been some assurance to him in those first few months after he left India. On the point about religion, Adams, like several over biographers, has failed to understand how Freemasonry distances itself from formal religion. A better interpretation of Kipling's early attraction to it, is that Freemasonry avoided the deep religious divisions that otherwise divided men in India, and was also one of the few meeting grounds where men of differing persuasions could meet without religious differences.

It is ironic that a man who guarded his privacy and disliked analysis of his work should have been subjected to so much scrutiny. Kipling wrote to Dunsterville (Stalky), who accepted office as the first President of the Kipling Society, " how would *you* like to be turned into an anatomical specimen before you are dead....?."[32]

MASONIC NOTES AND GLOSSARY

There appears to be a continuing interest in Kipling, his life and works and I hope this book will cover an aspect of his life and work that has so far only received cursory analysis, apart from a few specialist articles and one booklet. On the assumption that some non-Masonic Kipling readers may be interested to explore this side of the writer, I have described below a little of the history and background of Freemasonry and the Masonic rituals and procedures that are featured in Kipling's works.

Despite popular misconceptions, Freemasonry is not a secret society, but a society whose members have ways of recognizing each other that are only known to them. The details of the ceremonies are available in any decent public library. In recent years, English Freemasonry, headed by H.R.H. the Duke of Kent, the Grand Master of the United Grand Lodge of England, has encouraged the development of greater openness by members of the Craft. The 275th Anniversary of Grand Lodge (in which the author participated), was held at Earl's Court in 1992, and thousands of Masons and their partners from all over the world witnessed the ceremony. Considering how little time Kipling spent actively involved in Freemasonry, his knowledge was outstanding; but that is typical of the writer who not only paid endless attention to detail but had an encyclopedic memory to go with it.

It is always difficult to find a short definition of Freemasonry but in its simplest form it is an organization for men based on traditions, probably handed down from the old stonemasons' trade guilds, and which has as it basis the encouragement of brotherly love, charity and truth. It requires a belief in a deity, but does not belong to any specific religion. It is a meeting ground for men of all faiths.

The Origins of Freemasonry

Despite vast quantities of research, the origins of Speculative Freemasonry (in contrast to Operative Freemasonry) remain clouded in obscurity. The most popular view is that Masonry as we know it today was derived from the medieval trade guilds, especially those involved in building the great cathedrals of Europe in the Middle Ages. As young masons learnt their craft from the older builders, they were advanced from being apprentices until they became master masons, and at each stage of their training they were introduced to further technical secrets of their trade. These groups of stone masons toured Europe from the 11th century onwards. They devised Ancient Charges and Regulations to govern their trade. It is likely that they formed craft guilds and adopted the story of the building of the greatest structure referred to in the Bible - King Solomon's Temple at Jerusalem as the inspiration for their professional code. There is no significant recorded link between these men and modern (post 1717) Freemasonry in England, although in Scotland there is more evidence of the transition from local trade guilds that were gradually opened to non-masons in the seventeenth century.

In England the earliest recorded Freemason was Elias Ashmole (of the Oxford museum fame) who was initiated in 1646. Nothing is known about the Lodge that initiated him other than it met at Warrington in Lancashire After the first Grand Lodge was established in London in 1717, the institution grew quickly. It soon became highly structured, with Freemasonry spreading rapidly through Europe, with countries being broken down into provinces or Districts. From its early days, members could be of any religious persuasion. The only requirement was the belief in a Supreme Being.

In Europe, Eighteenth and Nineteenth century Freemasonry was strongly associated with the Enlightenment Movement. The academic Margaret Jacob wrote, "In its essential optimism Masonic literature is utopian: it looks to the secular and social order for perfectability. But in so looking, it exhibits a distinctly practical attitude. Although concerned with coherence and rationality of the ideal society, British Masonic utopian literature imagines that such order is in some sense possible." Such an assessment of its attraction would ring very true with Kipling.

The early history of English Freemasonry is quite turbulent as the first Grand Lodge split between two groups calling themselves the 'Antients' and 'Moderns', the division caused largely by differences over the form of ritual. Both groupings prospered, although with different systems, but eventually in 1813 they were reconciled and reunited under the title they have today: The United Grand Lodge of Antient, Free and Accepted Masons of England.

Today English Freemasonry is administered and governed from the offices of the United Grand Lodge in Great Queen Street in London. The country is divided into Provinces roughly equivalent to the old English counties and often follow the old county boundaries. The larger Provinces may have several hundred lodges and there are more than 7000 in the whole country. In addition, Grand Lodge also has authority over a number of District Grand Lodges in many overseas territories. There are almost a hundred other Grand Lodges world-wide recognized by our English Grand Lodge.

Becoming a Freemason

Most men become Freemasons after they are introduced to the Craft by a relative or friend. First they may meet a few members of the Lodge, often at a Ladies Night, and later have a formal interview to ensure that they understand what may be required of them, including the time commitment and cost. Many Lodges now hold Gentlemen's Evenings to explain to non-Masons what Freemasonry is about and to give them an opportunity to ask questions. After the prospective candidate has decided to join he will be formally proposed at a Lodge meeting and, if elected, a date for his initiation will be set. His proposer and seconder into the Lodge will brief him on what will be required of him at his initiation.

At that initiation the candidate will go through a ceremony when he pledges his agreement to the Rules of the Craft. He is then 'a Brother' and an Entered Apprentice.

Within a few months he will be "passed" to the Second Degree when he becomes known as a Fellow Craft. Finally, again usually a few months later, he is "raised" to the Third Degree and becomes a Master Mason. At each stage he is given simple tests and asked to confirm his loyalty to the institution. The speed at which he passes through these ceremonies will largely depend on how busy the Lodge is and whether there are other candidates who are also waiting to go through ceremonies. Once he is a fully fledged Master Mason he will also be asked to join the Lodge of Instruction or Rehearsal so that he may start to learn more about the ceremonies in anticipation of his own involvement.

Depending on the size of the Lodge the Master Mason would then start to proceed through the various offices of the Lodge, on average taking 10-15 years, when he will finally become the Worshipful Master of his Lodge and preside over it for a year. After he becomes a Master Mason he will start to learn some of the ritual so that by the time he becomes Worshipful Master he will be familiar with the work and be able to conduct the Lodge's ceremonies. During the year following his installation as Worshipful Master he will rule the Lodge and occupy what is known as the Chair of King Solomon. Some Masons have always found it harder than others to learn the ceremonies but there is no compulsion for them to do so. Some Masons prefer to only progress so far through the offices in the Lodge, but the majority do proceed to become Master of their Lodge. It is considered praiseworthy if a brother can learn a ceremony or parts of a ceremony, and can recite it without prompting. Kipling went through those three degree ceremonies in the year after he was initiated, but the only office he ever occupied formally was that of secretary - in all Lodges a pivotal position on which the administration and success of the Lodge may depend. The secretary plays a vital role but has no formal part in the ceremonial.

Freemasonry is explained to an initiate as "A system of morality, veiled in allegory and illustrated by symbols." The ceremonies, in which a candidate participates, all contain elements of the story of the building of King Solomon's Temple in Jerusalem and the murder of his principal architect Hiram Abiff. Part of this story is taken from the books of Kings and Chronicles in the Bible, and part is apocryphal. Hiram Abiff is murdered because he refuses, even under extreme duress, to disclose the secrets of his craft. His fidelity is the foundation of the moral code that Freemasonry employs. Death rather than dishonor is at the heart of this. At one time the vows that a new Mason took in each ceremony contained quite violent language, but those have been softened considerably in modern times. The other crucial vow relates to charity. Every new candidate is lectured on the virtues of charity and helping those less fortunate. At his initiation, a candidate is deprived of anything of value so that he is admitted into the Lodge "poor and penniless". This is to remind him to be conscious of others who may be in financial distress, and to help where he can.

Charity remains a significant part of Masonic life. Freemasons support the widows and children of their deceased brethren if they have fallen on straitened times but the scope of Masonic charity is much wider than that. In the U.K. the Grand Charity and other Masonic charities support not only the young, sick and elderly among Freemasons but provide tens of millions of pounds every year for a wide range of mainstream charities, including hospices, medical research at our teaching universities and an extended range of other charities. Grants are also made to assist catastrophes at home and abroad.

What is known as "the Craft" is the central degree in Freemasonry and splits into the three ceremonies detailed above. Although it is may be the most important, it is also only a small part of the whole range of Masonic orders. There are over thirty "side" or subsidiary orders, all recognized by Grand Lodge which brethren can join generally after they have become a Master Mason. Kipling joined two others. He became a Mark Mason. This is degree to which reference is also made in *The Man Who Would Be King*. He also joined another degree which is an offshoot of the Mark Degree, Royal Ark Mariners. Each degree is based upon different episodes in the Old Testament and has its own distinct ritual and ceremonies. Mark Masonry is concerned with the quarrying of the stones for the Temple. Royal Ark Mariners utilizes the story of Noah. Most Masonic degrees are open to members of all faiths, but there are also exclusively Christian degrees such as Rose Croix and Knights Templar, which have a New Testament source. Some enthusiastic Masons will join many of these other degrees, but many will never venture beyond the Craft and the membership of a single Craft lodge.

The ceremonies are all short plays or morality tales. The initiation ceremony is still virtually identical to that which Kipling had undergone in 1886. The candidate must also be at least 21, or a dispensation provided by the Lodge's governing body. In Kipling's case he was only 20. It is not uncommon for this to happen, especially if the candidate for initiation is the son of an existing member of the Lodge. At his initiation he will wear a Masonic apron for the first time – at that stage a pure white one

Each degree is separate and distinct, and has a different message or lesson for the candidate. In *The Man Who Would Be King* Dravot and Carnehan think that the natives they meet have been through the Second Degree ceremony, but not the Third. Once a candidate has been through the Third Ceremony he is a fully fledged member of the Lodge, and he will wear a blue apron of a Master Mason. Each year on the Installation of the new Worshipful Master, the junior Brother will be promoted up the ladder. Depending on his aptitude for the work of the Lodge, he will be given different tasks in the lodge ceremonies. He will progress through the different offices starting as a humble Steward, serving drinks and helping at the Festive Board, the dinner held after each Lodge meeting.

Normally on installation night those members (or more correctly Brethren) who have not been Master will be promoted to a higher office. Our new Brother having done his time as a Steward may then be promoted to Inner Guard. His job will then be to guard the door of the Lodge and identify anyone, especially latecomers, requiring admission. He also has a small role in the opening and closing ceremonies of the Lodge and the three main ceremonies. That will be his first speaking role in the Lodge and helps introduce younger members to the habit of participating in the ceremonies. (The one task that Kipling performed on his brief return to his Lodge in Lahore).

As the new Mason learns more, he will carry out the offices of Junior and Senior Deacon, where he will play an even more active part in the ceremonies, effectively acting as guide and mentor to newer candidates during the ceremonies. In many Lodges, at this stage of his career, he may become Secretary or Assistant Secretary of the Lodge. This is a crucial role in the whole administration of the Lodge. It is an indication of the respect in which the young Kipling was held that he was appointed to this office almost immediately. The Secretary and Assistant Secretary take all the minutes of both the main Lodge meeting and the meetings of officers and past masters which are usually held between meetings to handle the affairs of the Lodge. In addition, they will usually prepare the summons sent to member before each meeting, giving the agenda for the meeting. Nowadays this is usually computer generated and sent by email, but that is a recent change but nevertheless an indication that Freemasonry has kept up with modern technology The Secretary or his assistant will often arrange the catering for the Festive Board after the Lodge meeting, making sure that the caterer has the correct number. He will deal with all the correspondence coming to the Lodge – a not inconsiderable task as Grand Lodge, Provincial Grand Lodge and others will pour paper down on him. Increasingly, in modern times, the job of Secretary is taken by a Past Master who has retired from work and has the time to carry out these extensive duties. He will often take this role for many years.

The keen Mason will follow these appointments by undertaking the position of Junior Warden and then Senior Warden He must complete a year in at least one of these positions to qualify to eventually become Master of his Lodge. Normally the Senior Warden will be elected to follow Worshipful Master in the Chair at the conclusion of his year in office. The Master and the two Wardens rule the Lodge and occupy the three principal seats or thrones in the Lodge room at the east, west and south sides are each tasked with specific responsibilities in the Lodge.

The Wardens also have a speaking role in every ceremony. At an initiation, the Junior Warden will deliver a charge to the Initiate. If he demonstrates ability with the ritual he may well make himself noticed by the senior brethren and that later may involve promotion to Provincial Grand Lodge or later even to Grand Lodge. On installation night the new Master will be installed at a special ceremony usually under the beady eye of a senior Provincial Officer who may be the Provincial Grand Master or one of his deputies or assistants. The Provincial Representative would use this annual event to gauge the health of the Lodge, the quality of the ritual, and whether there are senior officers who might be suitable for Provincial office.

In the early days of Freemasonry, forms of Masonic ritual varied from place to place, despite attempts by Grand Lodge to standardize it. Eventually, in the early nineteenth century the Emulation Lodge of Improvement was formed. This exists up to the current day to encourage and assist Freemasons in the standard form of ritual and to perfect their practice of it. Although much rarer today, until the last fifty years, many Freemasons could enact a ceremony in Lodge requiring a feat of memory equivalent to an actor learning major role in a Shakespeare play. A Mason who could deliver a word-perfect ceremony to the Emulation Lodge of Improvement was awarded a silver matchbox. Emulation working is now used by most Lodges under the jurisdiction of the United Grand Lodge of England, although regional variations or minor departures from it are quite common. If one were to travel only a mile or so from the province of Warwickshire, where the writer resides, into the adjoining Province of Worcestershire, one would encounter many small differences in the way the ritual is portrayed, although the words do not vary. On my first visit to a French Lodge I found it easy to follow the ceremony, despite my indifferent French, as it was completely Emulation Working, whereas in Germany they use a totally different ritual and there I was completely at sea. There are many other versions of Masonic ritual around the world as can be seen from the references in *In The Interests of the Brethren*.

Kipling is only one of many famous men who became Freemasons, but more than most the Craft became deeply embedded in his literary output.

One final thought on Freemasonry —although it discourages political discussion among its members, it nevertheless has a strong association with freedom and democracy and it is no co-incidence that the only regimes that have ever banned or persecuted Freemasons are those which have banned other freedoms, such as the Nazis and Communists.

For anyone interested in researching Masonic history I can thoroughly recommend the marvellous Library and Museum at United Grand Lodge in Great Queen's Street in London. Not only does it have outstanding written resources but the Museum has a great range of artefacts including, incidentally, the Chippendale chairs belonging to my own Lodge, which was founded in 1733.

ENDNOTES

I have quoted from Charles Carrington's *Rudyard Kipling: His Life and Work*, the authorized biography first published in 1955 and later published in a revised and extended edition by Pelican Books in 1970, in the footnotes referred to as 'Carrington'.

I have also used the following abbreviations in the footnotes:

The Letters of Rudyard Kipling Volumes 1-6 Edited by Professor Thomas Pinney ('Pinney')

Something of Myself, - SOM

The Man Who Would Be King -TMWWBK

Debits and Credits- D & C

Kipling Journal – K.J.

Where I have quoted extensively from the short stories, I have not given individual page references.

Chapter One - Kipling's Own Story

1. The life of the four sisters is described in *A Circle of Sisters* by Judith Flanders (Penguin), 2002.
2. *Baa Baa Black Sheep*.
3. Louis L. Cornell , *Kipling in India* , Macmillan, 1966, pp.10-11.
4. Edmund Wilson, *The Kipling That Nobody Read* in *The Wound and the Bow*, Ohio University Press,1997, p.90.
5. SOM p.16.
6. Ibid. p.6.
7. Ibid. p.6.
8. Ibid. p.8.
9. Pinney Vol. 2 pp. 313-4.
10. Trix Fleming, *Some Childhood Memories of Rudyard Kipling*, Chambers Journal, 1939.
11. SOM pp.22-23.
12. *Stalky & Co.*
13. SOM p.36.
14. *The Light that Failed.*
15. The long letters that passed between Kipling and Edmonia Hill are in Pinney, Vol. 1 (1872-89).
16. Carrington, p.84, quoting from the Kipling papers to which he was given access by Elsie Bambridge.
17. *The Life of the Marquess of Ripon*, Lucien Wolf, Vol. 1, John Murray, London, 1921, p.287.
18. SOM p.64.
19. Ibid. p.56.
20. Ibid. p.67.
21. Ibid. pp.45-47.
22. Carrington, p.115.
23. *Plain Tales from the Hills*.
24. SOM pp.71-2.
25. *Soldiers Three*, A.H.Wheeler & Co's Indian Railway Library No.1, reprinted in facsimile in 1986 by the R.S.Surtees Society.
26. SOM p.74.
27. Cornell, p.165.
28. SOM p.78.

29. Ibid. p.80.
30. Carrington, p.179.
31. Ibid. pp.181-183.
32. Martin Seymour-Smith, *Rudyard Kipling*, Macmillan Papermac, 1990.
33. Adam Nicholson, *The Hated Wife: Carrie Kipling 1862-1939*, Short Books, 1999, p.23.
34. *Plain Tales from the Hills.*
35. SOM pp.100-101.
36. Henry James, quoted by Lord Birkenhead, p.134.
37. Nicholson, p.11.
38. Carrington, p.226.
39. Ibid. p.268.
40. Carrington, p.278.
41. David Gilmour, *The Long Recessional: The Imperial Life of Rudyard Kipling*, John Murray, 2002, p.122.
42. Ibid. p.127.
43. SOM p.148.
44. Ibid. p.152.
45. Lord Birkenhead, p.209.
46. Carrington, p.368.
47. Andrew Lycett, *Rudyard Kipling*, Weidenfeld & Nicholson, 1999, p.327.
48. Gilmour, p.160.
49. Carrington, p.384.
50. Ibid. p.447.
51. Carrington, p.455.
52. Lord Birkenhead, pp.247-248.
53. John Webb, *Rudyard Kipling: Man Poet and Mason*, Ian Allan Regalia, 1996, p.33.
54. Carrington, p.510.
55. Anne Chisholm & Michael Davie, *Beaverbrook: A Life*, Hutchinson, 1992, p.94.
56. Lilias Rider Haggard, *The Cloak That I Left*, Boydell Press, 1976, p.261.
57. Ibid. pp. 259-261.
58. Pinney Vol. 5 (1920-1931).
59. SOM p.204.

Chapter Two - Freemasonry In India and Kipling' Masonic Career and Connections

1. Rustum Sohrabji Sidhwa, *The Grand District Lodge of Pakistan 1869-1969*, printed by Feroz Sons Lahore Ltd., p.5.
2. Sidhwa as above.
3. Prosonno Coomer Dutt, *How Hindus were admitted into the Mysteries of Freemasonry*, Victor Printing Works, Calcutta, 1900.
4. See the website of the Grand Lodge of India.
5. Jessica Harland Jacobs, *Builders of the Empire: Freemasonry and British Imperialism 1/1/-1927*, University of North Carolina Press 2007, p.280.
6. Frank Karpiel, *Freemasonry, Colonialism and Indigenous Elite,* paper presented at Interactions: Regional Studies, Global Processes, Historical Analysis, Library of Congress, Washington D.C., 2001.
7. Robert Freke Gould, *The History of Freemasonry, Volume lll*, Grange Publishing Works, Edinburgh, 1980,
8. Sir George McMunn, *Rudyard Kipling: Craftsman*, Robert Hale and Company, London, 1937 p.76.
9. Dr. E.Karim, K.J. No.189 March 1974.
10. Ibid.
11. Harry Carr, *Kipling and the Craft*, Ars Quatuor Coronatorum (AQC), 1964 Vol. 77.
12. SOM p.51.
13. Ibid. pp.52-53.
14. Webb, p.19.
15. Pinney, Vol. 5, p.26.
16. Carrington, p. 106.
17. Ibid. p. 543.
18. Sidhwa, pp.40-41.
19. Webb, p.20.
20. Ibid. p. 20.
21. *Handbook of the District Grand Lodge of the Punjab* printed by W.Ball & Co, Lahore, 1888.
22. Sidhwa p.243.

23. Reports of the Trustees of the Punjab Masonic Institution, Lahore, 1886.
24. *Brief History of Lodge Independence with Philanthropy No.391*, Allahabad, The Pioneer Press, 1916.
25. Pinney, Vol.1, p.204.
26. Sidhwa, p.41.
27. Professor Pinney edited six volumes of Kipling's letters which were published between 1990 and 2004.
28. K.J. No. 022, June 1932, p.61.
29. Researching on the internet I discovered a paper by W.Bro. David Cameron P.G.S.W. of Grand River Lodge No.151 in Kitchener Ontario who kindly sent me a photograph of the gavel.(see below)
30. SOM p.55.
31. K.J. No. 47, October 1938, p.90.
32. Pinney Vol. 2, p.189.
33. Pinney Vol.3, p.237.
34. Ibid. Vol. 5 p.504.
35. The paper by W.Bro. Cameron can be found at www.waterloomasons.com
36. K.J. No. 163, September 1967, p.6.
37. See paper by W.Bro.William T. Brown of Kipling Newporton Lodge No.315 and the Irish Lodge of Research, 2003, available on the internet at http://homepage.eircom.net/~minoan/Lodge200/Kipling.
38. *Brief History of Lodge Independence with Philanthropy* as above.
39. Pinney, Vol.5, p.130.
40. Lord Ampthill's speech can be found in the Kipling Journal Issue No. 030, June 1934, p.56.

Chapter Three - Kipling's Philosophy

1. Christopher Hitchens, in an essay entitled *A Man of Permanent Contradictions*, Atlantic, June 2002.
2. In Pinney, Vol. 5, there are a number of long letters to Elsie.
3. SOM pp.208-210.
4. Ibid.
5. SOM p.210-211.

6. Terry Eagleton, *Literary Theory*, Blackwell, 2002, pp.27-32.
7. David Gilmour, p.5.
8. Seen by the author in the Kipling Archive at Sussex University,
9. Wording from the Emulation Ritual initiation.
10. Shamsul Islam, *Kipling's 'Law': A Study of his Philosophy of Life*, The Macmillan Press, 1975.
11. Ibid.p.9.
12. Ibid.p.144.
13. Ibid. p.106.
14 Ibid.p.144.
15. Carrington, p.332.

Chapter Four - The Early Stories

1. Lord Birkenhead, p.100.
2. J.M.S.Tompkins, *The Art of Rudyard Kipling*, University Paperbacks, 1959, p.112.
3. Pinney, Vol.1 p.151.
4. Charles Allen, *Kipling Sahib: India and the Making of Rudyard Kipling*, Abacus, 2007, p.277.
5. Andrew Lycett in Chapters 4-6 of his book describes in detail how Kipling's experiences in India are reflected in the early stories.
6. See Peter Hopkirk, *Quest for Kim*, University of Michigan Press, 1999, which describes the background to the Great Game.
7. Ben Macintyre, *Josiah the Great: The True Story of the Man Who Would be King*, Harper Perennial, London, 2004.
8. J.M.S.Tompkins, p.112.
9. Kingsley Amis, *Rudyard Kipling*, Thames and Hudson, 1986, p.62.
10. MWWBK
11. SOM p.42.
12. MWWBK
13. Ibid.

14. Ibid.
15. Ibid.
16. Ibid.
17. Ibid.
18. Ibid.
19. Ibid.
20. Ibid.
21. Cornell, footnote, p.163.
22. Edmund Wilson, *The Wound and the Bow*, Ohio University Press, 1997, p.130.
23. Charles Allen, pp.262-3.
24. *Soldiers Three*.

Chapter Five – Kim

1. Nirad C.Chaudhuri in an essay *The Finest Story About India- in English* in *Rudyard Kipling: the man, his work and his world*, edited by John Gross, Weidenfeld & Nicholson, 1972.
2. SOM p.40.
3. Angus Wilson, *The Strange Ride of Rudyard Kipling*, Penguin Books, 1979, pp.129-132.
4. Edward Said, Introduction to *Kim*, Penguin Books, 1987, p.10.
5. Malcolm Muggeridge, *Chronicles of Wasted Time*, Collins, 1972, p.94.
6. Karim K.J. No. 285, March 1998, p.32.
7. Charles Allen, pp. 214-215.
8. *Kim*.
9. Ibid.
10. Emulation Ritual.
11. *Kim*.
12. Ibid.
13. Harland-Jacobs, p.63.
14. *Kim*.
15. Ibid.
16. Peter Hopkirk, p.194.
17. Pinney, Vol. 2, P.313.
18. SOM, p.8.

Chapter Six - Debits And Credits

1. Pinney, Vol.5, p.207.
2. *The Irish Guards in the Great War,*2 Vols.
3. Angus Wilson, p.314.
4. Ibid.p.315.
5. Quarterly Communication of United Grand Lodge of England, 7th January 1918.
6. Petition in the Quarterly Communication dated 9th December 1914.
7. Details of this are in a letter from John Hamill, the Grand Secretary inspected in Grand Lodge files.
8. Quarterly Communication, Vol XVI, 1917
9. J.M.S.Tomkins, p.175.
10. Letter inspected by the author in Grand Lodge files.
11. *In the Interests of the Brethren.* In this chapter, unless there is an endnote, all quotations are from the stories described in this chapter.
12. The word ' Lewis' is used by Freemasons in two contexts. Firstly it is a device used by stonemasons to raise heavy stones. A miniature version is seen on the pedestal of the Senior Warden in a lodge room. The term is also used to describe a son, born of a Freemason .
13. The author made an extensive but unproductive search of Grand Lodge files for both the wartime period and the years immediately after the First World War.
14. Sandra Kemp, *Kipling's Hidden Narratives*, Basil Blackwell, 1998, p.75.
15. Shamsul Islam, p.45.
16. Lord Birkenhead, p.313.
17. Martin Seymour Smith, p.373.
18. J.M.S.Tomkins, p.175.
19. Arthur Machen's fictional story entitled *The Bowmen* was published in the Evening News in 1914 and appears to have been accepted as a true event.
20. George Saintbury first employed the term in an introduction he wrote to *Pride and Prejudice* in 1894.
21. Andrew Lycett, *Rudyard Kipling*, Weidenfeld & Nicholson,1999,pp.513-514.

22. K.J. No. 128, Dec.1958, p.11.
23. Carrington, p. 544.
24. Philip Mason, *Kipling: The Glass, the Shadow and the Fire*, Harper & Row, 1975, p.280.
25. Nicholas Freeling, *The Janeites*, Arcadia, 2002.
26. The Tichborne case was one of the most celebrated of Victorian trials when a penniless Australian tried to pass himself off as heir to an English fortune.
27. *Mary Postgate* is in *A Diversity of Creatures*.
28. *Limits and Renewals*.

Chapter Seven - Kipling's Poems: Masonic and Others

1. Andrew Rutherford in the Introduction to *Rudyard Kipling: War Stories and Poems*, OUP, 1990.
2. Pinney, Vol. 2 p.66 (footnote).
3. *The Oxford Companion to English Literature* edited by Margaret Drabble, Oxford, 5th Edn., 1985, p.53.
4. Handbook of the District Grand Lodge of Pakistan 1888.
5. Gilmour, p.120.
6. Kipling Society web site The New Readers' Guide: notes on *The Palace* by George Keiffer and Mary Hamer.
7. K.J. No. 90, July 1949, p.17.
8. Pinney, Vol.2 p.27.
9. Emulation Ritual.
10. Carrington, p.584.

Chapter Eight - Other Masonic References in Kipling's Work

1. Thomas Pinney, Introduction to *The Day's Work*, OUP, 1987, p.xxi.
2. Pinney, Vol. 5, p.270.
3. Carrington, p.86
4. Quoted by Anthony Julius in *T.S.Eliot, Anti-Semitism and Literary Form*, Cambridge University Press, 1985.
5. See the Kipling Society, New Readers' Guide notes on *The Bold Prentice*.

Chapter Nine- Other Writers Views on Kipling's Masonry

1. Somerset Maugham, *Points of View*, Heinemann, 1958, pp.155-157.
2. Lord Birkenhead, p.364.
3. Carrington, p.106.
4. Ibid.
5. Hilton Brown, *Rudyard Kipling*, Harper & Brothers, 1945.
6. Ibid.p.11.
7. Ibid.p95.
8. Ibid.p.96.
9. Ibid.p.96.
10. Ibid.p.98.
11. Masonic ritual from the Third Degree ceremony.
12. Andrew Rutherford, *Kipling's Mind & Art*.
13. W.L.Renwick in *Kipling's Mind & Art* ed. Andrew Rutherford, Oliver & Boyd, 1965, p.3.
14. Ibid.pp 9-10
15. Ibid.
16. Lionel Trilling in *Kipling's Mind & Art* as above, p.87.
17. Ibid.p.85.
18. George Shepperson in *Kipling's Mind & Art*, p.128.
19. Ibid.
20. Noel Annan in *Kipling's Mind & Art*, p.116.
21. Sir George McMunn, *Rudyard Kipling: Craftsman*, Robert Hale and Company, 1937, pp.76-77.
22. John Raymond in *Rudyard Kipling: the man, his work and his world*, edited by John Gross, Weidenfeld & Nicholson, p.148.
23. Martin Seymour-Smith, Foreword to the Second Edition, 1990.
24. Seymour-Smith, p.160.
25. Ibid. p.373.
26. Philip Mason, p.25.
27. Sandra Kemp, p.74.
28. Lycett

29. Thomas Pinney in the Introduction to *The Day's Work*, OUP, 1987, p.xxi.
30. Andrew Lycett, p.473.
31. Jad Adams, p.29.
32. Pinney, Vol.5. p.393.

INDEX

BIBLIOGRAPHY

A Brief History of Lodge Independence with Philanthropy No.391, The Pioneer Press, Allahabad, 1916.

Adams, Jad *Kipling*, Haus Books, London, 2005.

Allen, Charles *Kipling Sahib: India and the Making of Rudyard Kipling*, Abacus, 2008.

Amis, Kingsley *Rudyard Kipling*, Thames & Hudson, 1986.

Ankers, Arthur R. *The Pater: John Lockwood Kipling His Life and Times 1837-1911*, Pond View Books, 1988.

Birkenhead, Lord *Rudyard Kipling*, W.H.Allen ,1980.

Carrington, Charles *Rudyard Kipling, His Life and Work*, Macmillan, 1955.

Chisholm, Anne and Davy, Michael *Beaverbrook: A Life,* Hutchinson, London, 1992.

Cornell, Louis L. *Kipling in India*, Macmillan, 1966.

Dalrymple, William *White Mughals*, Flamingo, 2003.

Dutt, Prosonno Coomer *How Hindus were Admitted into the Mysteries of Freemasonry*, Victor Printing Works, Calcutta, 1900.

Fido, Martin *Rudyard Kipling*, The Viking Press, New York, 1974.

Gilbert, Elliott L. *The Good Kipling; Studies in the Short Story*, Manchester University Press, 1972.

Gilmour, David *The Long Recessional : The Imperial Life of Rudyard Kipling*, John Murray, 2002.

Gross, John (Ed.) *Rudyard Kipling, The man his work and his world,* Weidenfeld & Nicholson, London, 1972.

Harland-Jacobs, Jessica *Builders of Empire: Freemasonry and British Imperialism 1717-1927*, University of North Carolina Press, 2007.

Hopkirk, Peter *Quest for Kim*, University of Michigan Press, 1999.

Islam, Shamsul *Kipling's 'Law', A Study of his Philosophy of Life*, Macmillan, 1975.

Jacob, Margaret C. *Living the Enlightenment, Freemasonry and Politics in Eighteenth Century Europe*, Oxford University Press, 1991.

Karling, Daniel (Ed) *Rudyard Kipling, A Critical Edition of the Major Works*, Oxford University Press, 1999.

Kemp, Sandra *Kipling's Hidden Narratives*, Basil Blackwell, 1988.

Kipling's India with an Introduction by Khushwant Singh, Roli Books, 2001.

Lycett, Andrew *Rudyard Kipling*, Weidenfeld & Nicholson, 1999.

Macdonald, Meryl *The Long Trail, Kipling Round the World*, Tideway House, 1999.

Macintyre, Ben *Josiah the Great,* Harper Perennial, London, 2004.

Mason, Philip *Kipling: The Glass, the Shadow and the Fire*, Harper & Row, New York, 1975.

Maugham, W.Somerset *Points of View*, Heinemann, London, 1958.

Pinney, Thomas (Ed.) *The Letters of Rudyard Kipling, Volumes 1 -6* Palgrave Macmillan, 1990-2004.

Ricketts, Harry *Rudyard Kipling, A Life*, Carroll & Graf, 1999.

Rutherford, Andrew (Ed.) *Kipling's Mind and Art*, Oliver & Boyd, 1965.

Seymour Smith, Martin *Rudyard Kipling*, Macdonald, 1989.

Sidhwa, Rustam Sohrabji *District Grand Lodge of Pakistan 1869-1969*, Lahore 1970.

Stewart, J.I.M. *Rudyard Kipling*, Dodd, Mead & Co, 1966.

Tompkins,J.M.S. *The Art of Rudyard Kipling*, Methuen & Co Ltd, London, 1965.

Webb, John Rudyard *Kipling, Man, Poet, Mason*, Ian Allan Regalia, Surrey, 1996.

Wilson, Angus *The Strange Ride of Rudyard Kipling*, Penguin Books, 1979.

BOOKS BY RUDYARD KIPLING

This is not an exhaustive list of Kipling's work but contains those works of interest to readers of this book and works that are quoted in this book. I have used the date of the edition I have used rather than the date of original publication

Captains Courageous, Macmillan & Co, London, 1922.

Debits and Credits, Macmillan & Co, London, 1926.

Kim, Penguin Classics, with an introduction by Edward Said, 2000.

Rewards and Fairies, Macmillan & Co, London, 1922.

The Day's Work, Oxford University Press, with an Introduction by Prof. Thomas Pinney, 1987.

Something of Myself: For My Friends Known and Unknown, Macmillan and Co, London 1937.